Sexual Fitness

Complete Vitality

FITNESS, HEALTH & NUTRITION

Sexual Fitness

Complete Vitality

Time-Life Books, Alexandria, Virginia

CONSULTANTS FOR THIS BOOK

Barbara DeBetz, M.D., is an Assistant Professor of Psychiatry at Columbia University College of Physicians and Surgeons, a practicing psychiatrist in New York City and a Diplomate of the American Board of Psychiatry and Neurology. An expert in the treatment of sexual dysfunction, she is the author of several books, including *Erotic Focus,* as well as numerous articles for magazines and medical journals.

Ann Grandjean, Ed.D., is Associate Director of the Swanson Center for Nutrition, Omaha, Neb.; chief nutrition consultant to the U.S. Olympic Committee; and an instructor in the Sports Medicine Program, Orthopedic Surgery Department, University of Nebraska Medical Center.

Myron Winick, M.D., is the R.R. Williams Professor of Nutrition, Professor of Pediatrics, Director of the Institute of Human Nutrition, and Director of the Center for Nutrition, Genetics and Human Development at Columbia University College of Physicians and Surgeons. He has served on the Food and Nutrition Board of the National Academy of Sciences and is the author of many books, including *Your Personalized Health Profile.*

The following consultants helped design the exercises in this book:

Marian E. Dunn, Ph.D., is Director and Clinical Associate Professor of Psychiatry at the Center for Human Sexuality at the State University of New York Health Science Center in Brooklyn, N.Y. She is also certified as a sex therapist and therapy supervisor by the American Association of Sex Educators, Counselors and Therapists.

Jessica Wolf is a certified Alexander teacher at the American Center for the Alexander Technique in New York City. She is also a certified Movement Analyst at the Laban Institute. In addition to maintaining a private practice, she teaches at colleges throughout the United States.

For information about any Time-Life book please call 1-800-621-7026, or write:
Reader Information
Time-Life Customer Service
P.O. Box C-32068
Richmond, Virginia 23261-2068

Library of Congress Cataloging-in-Publication Data
Sexual fitness: complete vitality.
p.   cm. — (Fitness, health & nutrition)
Includes index.
ISBN 0-8094-6110-2
1. Sex. 2. Physical fitness. 3. Exercise.
I. Time-Life Books. II. Series:
Fitness, health, and nutrition.
RA788.S478   1988
613.7—dc19   88-9405
                CIP

This book is not intended as a substitute for the advice of a physician. Readers who have or suspect they may have specific medical problems, expecially those involving their sexual health, should consult a physician or certified therapist about any suggestions made in this book. Readers beginning a program of strenuous physical exercise are also urged to consult a physician.

CONTENTS

CHAPTER ONE

Fitness and Sexuality

*The links among exercise, libido
and sexual response*

The benefits of being physically fit, as confirmed by many studies of the effects of exercise, range from a stronger heart to reduced psychological stress. Recently, a number of studies have indicated what some advocates of exercise have long asserted: that exercise can improve the quantity and quality of sexual activity. This book examines the physiological relationship between exercise and sexual behavior, looks at other factors that affect sexual desire and shows you exercise routines that you and your partner can perform together. Of course, as common sense — backed by scientific studies — indicates, a fulfilling sexual experience is not only a physical event, but a complex emotional and psychological one that requires intimacy as well as ardor. Therefore, in addition to exercises for fitness, the book provides physical routines designed to promote sensual communication through increased touching, which researchers have found is one of the best ways to enhance intimacy and add vitality to a couple's sexual relationship.

Exercise and Sexual Desire

Frequency per month

15

10

5

20 MINUTES
OF EXERCISE DAILY

40 MINUTES
OF EXERCISE DAILY

■ Sexual activity
■ Desired sexual activity

This graph shows the results of a study examining the link between recreational exercise and the sex drive. Those who exercised an average of 40 minutes a day had about twice the sexual activity and about twice as much desire for sex as the people who exercised 20 minutes a day. The 250 men and women in the study participated in walking, running, racquet sports, biking, swimming and weight lifting, among other activities.

What is sexual fitness?

Being sexually fit means being aware of — and utilizing — the benefits of physical fitness and sensual ways of touching to improve your sexual health and pleasure. Sex, after all, involves strong, vigorous movements; building up your aerobic endurance — your body's capacity to take in and use oxygen to power itself — as well as your muscular strength will improve your ability to perform these movements. Being physically fit contributes to sexual pleasure in two other ways as well: It can help you develop a more positive self-image, particularly with respect to how you feel about your body, and it can improve your ability to cope with stress-related tension that may inhibit sexual desire and performance.

Touch is another important element in sexual fitness. Besides developing your ability to give pleasure, learning to touch your partner sensitively and in a variety of ways increases your feelings of emotional intimacy and communication. The sensory stimulation produced by touch conveys feelings of empathy and tenderness that enhance sexual satisfaction and cannot be communicated adequately any other way.

Can being physically fit really improve your sex life?

Because sex entails interaction of the mind and body to such a great extent, it is difficult to assess its quality objectively. However, several studies do indicate that people who exercise regularly tend to be more active sexually than those who are sedentary. In one study, researchers compared the level of sexual activity found in groups of sedentary subjects with a group of male and female swimmers over the age of 25 who race in organized competition. They found that the swimmers reported a higher frequency of sexual intercourse than the sedentary people. Similarly, a survey of 155 members of recreational exercise groups revealed that men who were the most physically active maintained the most active sex lives. Another study that looked at more than 600 male heart patients showed that an exercise program produced a 16 percent increase in their frequency of intercourse. And in a study of women aged 22 to 60 who took an aerobic dance class three times week, researchers found that after three months the women reported an average 30 percent increase in frequency of sexual activity.

Of course, more sex does not necessarily mean better sex, but such a correlation has turned up. In the study of swimmers, those who were physically active also reported a greater enjoyment of sex than their sedentary counterparts.

In what ways can exercise benefit sexual response?

Although there has been no scientifically proven direct effect of exercise on sexual activity, studies of the physiological systems that contribute to sexuality suggest that the effects of exercise are beneficial. A great deal is now known about the changes that occur in the human body during sexual activity, thanks in large part to the work of Dr. William Masters and Virginia Johnson, the influential sex researchers and therapists who in the 1960s first studied sex under laboratory conditions. One of the most significant responses triggered by sexual arousal is increased blood flow to the genitals, which produces erections in men and thickening, swelling and lubrication of the genital tissues in women. This pooling of blood, which is called vasocongestion, is accompanied by a temporary increase in blood pressure, as well as a rise in heart rate (which may double) and in respiration rate.

The process of vasocongestion depends upon the blood vessels that deliver blood to your genitals being healthy and clear of obstructions. In men, blockages and narrowing of arteries can limit blood flow to the penis (as well as to other areas of the body) and have been linked to difficulties in achieving and maintaining erections. Exercise that is aerobic — that raises your heart rate continuously for a sustained period, such as when you run, bicycle or swim laps — has been shown to help guard against these conditions as well as to improve the efficiency of your cardiovascular system. The long-term benefits of these exercises include a reduction in resting heart rate, which is an indication that your heart can pump more blood per contraction and is less taxed by the demands of physical activity. These and other changes that researchers have attributed to regular exercise — and that were observed in several of the studies cited above — would appear to help ensure and possibly improve proper sexual functioning as well as your overall health.

Are there exercises that can improve sexual performance?
Because many of the body's major muscles are used during sex, developing their tone and flexibility can help sexual performance. Conditioning the musculature of the stomach, hips and thighs is especially useful, since sexual activity almost always involves intensive use of these areas of the body. There are also exercises you can perform to strengthen the internal pelvic muscles that play an important role in orgasm. Both types of exercises are covered in Chapter Two of this book.

But you should also bear in mind that therapists and sex counselors feel that an overemphasis on performance can hamper enjoyment of sex. Indeed, when people feel they must perform in a certain way, they often have difficulty functioning at all. Sex therapists typically try to assure couples who are experiencing sexual difficulties that a sexual interlude does not have to include intercourse to be satisfying, nor does it have to result in orgasm.

What else can couples do to remove performance pressure from their sexual relationship?
Many sex therapists believe that nonsexual touching — touching as a pleasurable activity in and of itself, or touching for affection rather than as foreplay for sexual intercourse — is a valuable addition to a sexual relationship. This type of physical intimacy, which includes holding hands and hugging, enhances emotional communication between the partners in a relationship. And emotional communication, which involves understanding each other's needs, problems and moods, is necessary for a fulfilling sex life. Affectionate, nonsexual touching that takes place daily creates an atmosphere conducive to relaxation and pleasure.

The touching exercises shown in Chapter Three represent touching that is sexual but does not necessarily focus on sexual intercourse as its ultimate goal. These touching exercises are similar to the techniques Masters and Johnson and other therapists employ, but the techniques are not just a therapeutic method. Because they are often slower and more relaxed than touching that serves as foreplay for sexual intercourse, touching exercises can greatly increase your awareness of physical sensation, as each partner learns what kinds of stroking and touching he or she finds most pleasurable. The exercises that concentrate on various aspects of sensuality can be used by any couple to add an extra dimension of pleasure and zest to their sexual relationship.

The Training Effect

Frequency of intercourse per month

15

12

9

6

3

3   6   9

MONTHS OF
TRAINING

Does the human body have particular erogenous zones that can intensify sexual arousal and response?
Generally, certain areas of the human body tend to be more sensitive to sexual arousal and response than others. These include the lips, ears, tip of the nose, breasts and genital area, though the degree of sensitivity varies from person to person. However, no one particular spot is guaranteed to lead to arousal when touched; the fact is, almost any part of your body can be caressed in such a way as to arouse you if you are in a receptive frame of mind.

What physiological mechanisms have an effect on sexual desire?
According to some researchers, the level of testosterone in the blood seems to influence sexual desire, or libido. Although testosterone is sometimes called the male hormone because its production is associated with the development of secondary sex characteristics in men, both men's and women's bodies secrete this chemical. In men, testosterone is produced in the testes, while women produce it in their adrenal glands and their ovaries. At least one study has indicated that

For some people, the improvements in vitality from a training program carry over into sex. In one study, men who completed a nine-month running program had sexual intercourse more than 12 times a month at the end of the program, compared with about seven times monthly before beginning training, as the chart above shows. In a separate study of 25 women, the frequency of sexual activity rose 30 percent after a three-month aerobic dance program.

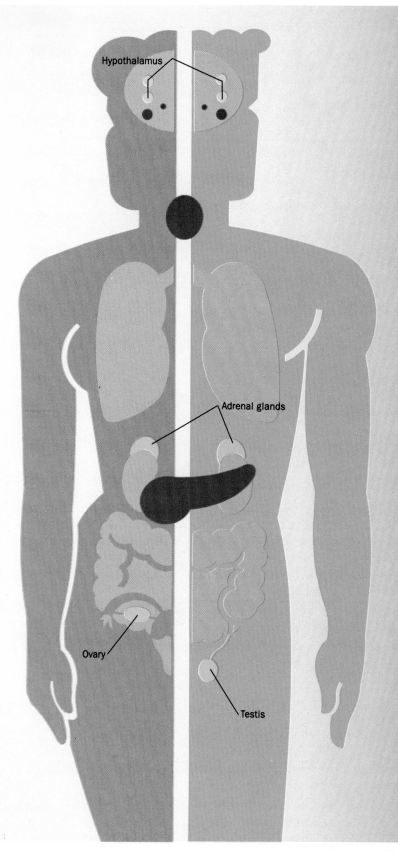

Hypothalamus

Adrenal glands

Ovary

Testis

The Physiology of Arousal

Human sexual response emerges from a complex network of physiological and psychological factors. Among the key factors in libido for both sexes is the hormone testosterone, which is produced by the body's endocrine system, as shown at left. Testosterone production occurs in the testes in men; in women testosterone is produced in the ovaries and adrenal glands. The control mechanism is in the hypothalamus in the brain.

Exercise can affect testosterone levels both positively and negatively. Scientific studies have established that 15-20 minutes of moderate exercise can significantly increase the production of testosterone in your body. Prolonged strenuous exercise, however, such as running a marathon, can lower it. Clearly, exercise-induced changes can affect your interest in sex.

Stress can also affect your sexual response, almost always negatively: Researchers have found that severe or prolonged stress lowers testosterone production. This may explain why many people experience a drop in sexual desire when they are under stress and, conversely, a boost in sexual desire with regular, stress-relieving workouts.

relatively short periods of strenuous exercise — exercise that lasts 45 minutes or less — produce an increase in blood levels of testosterone and may be linked to an increase in sexual desire. Research indicates that other hormones within the body, including estrogen (the hormone linked to secondary female characteristics), also affect sexual desire and response, although the complicated interaction of these hormones is not completely understood. Furthermore, for people who do not have an underlying pathological condition that affects their sexual function, the psychological factors that affect sexual response are more important.

Does that mean sexual desire is more an emotional than a physical phenomenon?

For most people, sexual desire is inextricably linked to their emotional condition. Feelings of attraction for another person can stimulate an emotional response that leads to increased sexual desire. But these psychological factors are hard to document in a scientifically consistent manner. They vary greatly from person to person, and individuals frequently experience wide swings in sexual desire. Often the causative emotional factors are not intrinsically sexual: Two of the most frequent reasons cited for a dampening of sexual desire, for example, are marital discord and boredom, both of which can stem from many causes. Furthermore, there is no widely accepted benchmark for assessing a person's level of desire. Frequency of intercourse, for example, is not necessarily a good gauge of sexual desire. The amount of activity that one couple finds fulfilling may be inadequate for another couple who have different expectations. As a result of all these uncertainties, many psychologists now take the position that an acceptable level of desire and activity is whatever keeps a couple satisfied.

At the same time, a persistent lack of desire — which clinically is known as Inhibited Sexual Desire, or ISD — has emerged in the past few years as one of the most common of all sexual complaints, and one of its leading causes appears to be stress. According to clinicians, the type of stress that disrupts sexual desire most often originates in depression, anxiety, anger or guilt, or in concerns about self-image or body-image.

Can exercise help to restore or intensify sexual desire?

Anyone who suffers a prolonged loss of libido should consult a physician, since chronic and acute illnesses, certain medications for those illnesses or a wide range of endocrine disorders may be responsible. And many instances of diminished desire may require the help of a therapist who specializes in sexual problems. But if your loss of libido is connected to stress, research shows that an exercise program can alleviate or ameliorate these kinds of problems. For example, a study of college students enrolled in a cardiovascular fitness program showed that these students displayed a greater decrease in anxiety than a control group did. Exercise has also been found to have a positive effect on individuals who suffer from depression, and there have been a number of studies demonstrating a positive relationship between physical fitness and general psychological well-being.

Because a consistent exercise program can firm your muscles, help you lose weight and generally improve your physical appearance, it can also enhance your body-image, another psychological component of sexuality. A number of psychologists have reported that many people who are not satisfied with their sex lives are also not comfortable with their bodies. In one study, overweight adults were asked how they would see themselves after losing weight, and among their responses they indicated anticipating a much higher level of sexual satisfaction. In addition to building confidence about your appearance, exercise also makes you more aware of your body and how it responds, and therefore you are more likely to be in tune with what pleases you physically during sexual activity.

Because alcohol has the ability to relax you, can it help make sex more pleasurable?

In moderate amounts, alcohol may stimulate sexual arousal and diminish inhibitions or anxieties. But physiologically, alcohol acts to hamper sexual vitality. Alcohol is a depressant, and as such it slows down reflexes, decreases physical sensation and can cause impotence in men. Alcohol consumption, even from a single bout of heavy drinking, has been shown to decrease the production of testosterone. Therefore, if you want optimal vitality during sex, it is best to limit your consumption to one or two drinks prior to sexual activity or to abstain from drinking. Alcohol may have toxic effects on the parts of the brain that regulate the release of sex-related hormones. Up to 80 percent of males who are heavy drinkers experience impotence, sterility or loss of sexual desire. In women, alcoholism has been linked to difficulty in becoming sexually aroused and in achieving orgasm.

Are there any effective aphrodisiacs or specific nutrients that can enhance sexual fitness?

As far as food or drink is concerned, there is no such thing as an aphrodisiac. But some reputed aphrodisiacs may contain minerals that are related to the proper functioning of your sexual organs and, as explained in Chapter Four, that are necessary to the health of your senses. Oysters, for instance, long considered an aphrodisiac, contain zinc, which affects your sense of smell and taste as well as your fertility. Since a person's state of mind plays a strong role in his or her sexual life, consuming a substance believed to be an aphrodisiac may enhance sexual performance, but the substance itself has no effect.

Can testosterone supplements increase libido?

Although some doctors prescribe testosterone supplements for their male patients with Inhibited Sexual Desire, research shows that for those men with normal blood levels of this hormone, testosterone supplements are ineffective. However, men whose testosterone levels are abnormally low — a rare condition — can benefit from testosterone therapy. While the hormone has no effect on erections or orgasm, testosterone deficiency can cause absent or diminished libido; hormone replacement in this case can often restore interest in sexual activity.

The same is true for women. A recent study done in Canada of about 250 women who had become postmenopausal as a result of surgery looked at the effects of testosterone supplements on libido. Researchers found that women who received testosterone preparations or testosterone combined with estrogen had much higher levels of libido than women who received placebos or estrogen alone. The therapy restored their libido to levels equal to or higher than they did prior to their surgery.

Because of its potential side effects, testosterone therapy has to be conducted under close medical supervision, and it should be discontinued promptly if it does not produce beneficial results.

How does aging affect your sexual vitality?

Generally, men's sexual interest peaks when they are in their teens or early twenties. After those ages, male sexual response tends to slow down. Older men need more direct stimulation in order to achieve and maintain erections and to reach ejaculation than young men do, and they experience longer refractory periods, the amount of time between erections. Also, both the angle of their erections and the force of their ejaculation is lessened as they grow older.

Women, too, take longer to get excited and their orgasmic phase tends to shorten, with the decrease usually beginning around the age of 50. However, sexual desire in women generally does not decline as they get older. As a matter of fact, according to researchers, postmenopausal women retain their responsiveness as long as they have a satisfactory sex partner. And, in their later years, some women are reported to enjoy sex more, since that part of their libido controlled by testosterone continues, and the desire-suppressing effects of the premenopausal hormones estrogen and progesterone are gone.

Studies by Masters and Johnson indicate that sexual activity for men and women can continue at least into their eighties, if not beyond. Obviously, not everyone will experience an active sex life that long. Physical problems like diabetes, arteriosclerosis, chronic liver disease and low thyroid activity may cause impotence in men and disrupt the normal blood levels of sex hormones in both sexes, and can therefore interfere with your sex life at any age. But in the absence of physical illness, researchers have never found an age beyond which sexual activity invariably comes to an end. For most men and women, any decline in sex drive that accompanies aging is primarily a consequence of psychological factors such as stress or expectations that sexual frequency should decline with advanced age,

Although a couple's sexual problems are among the leading causes for seeking marriage counseling, sexual satisfaction ranks high among couples happily married for more than a decade, according to one survey. Researchers asked 350 couples wed for at least 15 years to explain why their marriages had lasted so long. Seventy percent reported overall satisfaction with their sex life. Among other reasons listed for marital success were mutual friendship and admiration, compatibility and respect for the marriage vows.

Sources of Dysfunction

RECREATIONAL DRUGS

HYPERTENSION MEDICATION

ALCOHOL

ANTI-DEPRESSANTS

Male sexual dysfunction is commonly attributed to exhaustion, stress or emotional problems. But researchers have found that substances like those in the illustration at right can also interfere with the male sexual response. Frequently, the problem can be remedied by switching to another brand of medication. In the case of overdoing alcohol or marijuana and other recreational drugs, the best solution is to break the habit.

rather than the result of physiological changes. This decline in sex drive is not a problem when it occurs equally in both partners.

Exercise may help forestall a drop in sex drive and desire. Older adults who exercise regularly appear to maintain a relatively high level of sexual interest and activity. In the study of swimmers over 25 cited earlier, the frequency of intercourse among those who were over 60 was typical of nonswimmers 20 to 40 years younger.

Will abstinence from sexual activity decrease your sexual fitness? While forgoing exercise may lower your physical fitness, abstaining from sexual relations will not harm your sexual fitness. People practice temporary celibacy for a large number of reasons. These include the need to devote more time to business matters, artistic endeavors and scholastic activities, or to deal with psychological disruptions caused by emotional turmoil connected to the death of a loved one or the ending of a relationship. Some therapists believe that abstinence from sexual relations can serve a useful purpose. It allows you to analyze your relationships from a more detached perspective. And in the case of stress caused by a traumatic emotional event, abstinence can provide an emotional breathing space that allows you to recover from the stressful occurrence.

In older people, sustained periods of abstinence can result in diminished sexual fitness, while maintaining an active sex life can help preserve healthy functioning of the sexual organs. For example, women who have sex or masturbate at least once a week can slow down changes in vaginal tissue, such as a loss of elasticity and lubrication, associated with aging.

Can exercise become a substitute for sex?

Such a phenomenon has been documented, but it is potentially a problem only among people who are devoting a great deal of time to exercise. One study found that a small percentage of male runners who consistently ran more than 40 miles a week claimed that, given a choice, they would rather give up sex than give up running. The decreased interest in sex among dedicated exercisers is probably due to overall fatigue, depressed blood levels of testosterone and emotional obsession with exercise. A study of male ultramarathoners who ran in a race covering 250 miles in 15 days found that running long distances decreased testosterone in the blood by about 30 percent. In female athletes, research has linked strenuous exercise and a very low percentage of body fat to menstrual irregularities and disruption of normal hormone production, both of which may be associated with decreased sexual desire. For some of these people, the obsessive need to work out constantly leaves no room in their lives for a strong sexual relationship. Most men and women who exercise, of course, do not fall into this category, and for them working out regularly can only help increase sexual vitality.

What benefits are there to working out with your sex partner?

Working out together has several advantages. For one thing, it helps you stick to a consistent exercise program because of your commitment to your partner. A partner also provides motivation and support during a workout, getting you to push yourself harder. Partner exercises like those in Chapter Two may even enable you to do exercises that you would not or could not do on your own. Also, many people find that solo exercise programs cut into the time they spend with their families and partners; working out together gives you an opportunity for more shared time. A guide to the partner exercises in this book is on page 25.

Becoming Sexually Informed

Part of achieving sexual fitness is being well-informed. Otherwise, you may cling to myths that can interfere with your pleasure and openness in a sexual relationship. The topics covered in the statements at right are common areas of confusion reported by sex researchers and therapists. The rest of this chapter presents specific information on birth control and sexually transmitted diseases, and guides you to the exercises in the chapter that follow.

Common Misconceptions

1 **To be satisfactory, a sexual experience must end in orgasm.**

There is no reason why sexual arousal must lead to climax. And in fact, focusing sexual activity toward orgasm can intensify performance anxieties and also routinize a sexual relationship if both partners rely on position and techniques they know will lead to orgasm. Sex therapists often suggest that people who have problems with arousal can benefit from sex that does not culminate in orgasm, but anyone can expand sexual pleasure in this way. For exercises that focus on sensual rather than sexual touching, see Chapter Three.

2 **Impotence in men is almost always caused by psychological problems.**

The frequency of impotence and its causes are matters of debate among researchers. Nearly all men have difficulty achieving erections at some point in their lives, but an estimated 5 to 7 percent of American men have recurring problems with potency. For many years, health professionals emphasized psychological causes of these problems, ranging from stress and anxiety to various neuroses. But researchers have found that impotence can also result from such physiological conditions as diabetes — for which impotence is sometimes the first symptom — arteriosclerosis and alcoholism. Prescription drugs for hypertension, depression, ulcers and glaucoma can also induce impotence. Any treatment for impotence, therefore, should begin with a physical examination and a review of one's medical history.

3 **Masturbating after you are married probably indicates sexual or marital problems.**

While it is often assumed that people who are happily married do not masturbate, the practice is actually quite common, according to sex researchers Masters and Johnson. One study of young married couples found that 72 percent of husbands masturbated an average of 24 times a year, and 68 percent of wives masturbated an average of 10 times a year. Other studies of older married couples report that the practice continues to be common in later married life. For many people, masturbating is not simply or necessarily an alternative to sex with a partner, but it becomes an additional part of your sex life, to be enjoyed for itself and as a way of employing fantasy to add variety.

4 Douching is a good way for women to maintain sexual hygiene.

Except when a doctor prescribes it, douching regularly is not necessary to maintain cleanliness. The acidity of normal vaginal secretions helps keep the area free of infection. If improperly done, douching may be dangerous because it can force air or fluid into the uterus. Douching does not work as a method of birth control, since sperm swim so fast that even douching immediately after intercourse is usually too late to prevent some sperm from passing through the cervix.

5 Sex can impair (or improve) your athletic performance.

For many years coaches told athletes not to have sex the night before a game, based on the belief that having intercourse saps one's energy. Some athletes on the other hand believe that having sex before a game or meet will enhance their performance. In fact, sex has no effect one way or another on athletic performance. Sex uses up no more calories than are required for walking, and unless you substitute sex for adequate rest, there is no reason it should wear you out. If sex helps you to relax, fine, but there is no evidence that it is superior to other methods of relaxation.

6 Nowadays, except for AIDS, Sexually Transmitted Diseases can be cured easily.

It is true that some Sexually Transmitted Diseases are fairly easy to treat. Common strains of gonorrhea and syphilis, for example, are caused by organisms that can be treated effectively with penicillin. However, new strains of gonococcus, the bacteria that causes gonorrhea, have emerged that are resistant to penicillin and to other standard antibiotics, and doctors have had far more trouble curing the disease caused by these newer strains. Other diseases, such as herpes and genital warts, are caused by viruses, which cannot be combatted by antibiotics. In fact, there is no cure for herpes, though there are drugs that will alleviate the discomfort it produces. Another factor complicating treatment of various Sexually Transmitted Diseases is that the symptoms they produce are often difficult to detect. Medical experts, therefore, increasingly emphasize prevention as the best way of protecting yourself. For information on the protective measures available, see page 23.

Choosing a Contraceptive

Except for abstinence, the ideal birth control method — 100 percent safe, 100 percent effective and easy to use without interfering with the sex act — has yet to be found. Although the variety of contraceptives may be greater than ever, choosing among them involves more than weighing their risks or inconveniences against their effectiveness in preventing pregnancy. Most notably, condoms are widely promoted because they also significantly reduce the chance of contracting Sexually Transmitted Diseases. (For a full discussion of STDs, see the following two pages.) And oral contraceptives, which pose a multitude of risks for certain women, particularly those who smoke, are now known to protect against some types of cancers.

The chart opposite compares the most common types of reversible birth control methods. The figures given for effectiveness reflect the actual failure rates of each method, based on records of use over time. These statistics take into account accidents, such as forgetting to take the pill or removing the diaphragm within six hours of intercourse, and are therefore somewhat higher than a "theoretical failure rate," which is based on hypothetical perfect use. An effectiveness rating of 95 percent means that during one year, five women of every 100 using that method of birth control became pregnant.

Sterilization is excluded from the chart because most forms are not reversible, and the rhythm method and coitus interruptus are excluded because of their high failure rates.

TYPE	EFFECTIVENESS
Birth Control Pill	• 98% (combination pill, with synthetic versions of the female hormones estrogen and progesterone) • 97% ("minipill," with synthetic progesterone only)
Condom	Nearly 90%; when female partner uses spermicide, close to 100%
Diaphragm	90-98% when used with spermicide
Vaginal sponge	85-90%
Intrauterine device (IUD)	95%
Spermicidal cream, jelly, foam, suppository	70-80% when used alone; recommended for use with condom or diaphragm, which increases effectiveness to nearly 100%

ADVANTAGES	DISADVANTAGES
• Results in lighter, shorter, more regular menstrual periods; decreases or eliminates menstrual cramps and may relieve pre-menstrual syndrome. • Decreases the risk of pelvic inflammatory disease, fibrocystic breast disease and benign ovarian cysts. • Estrogen/progesterone pill protects against ovarian and uterine cancer.	• Must be taken on a regular daily schedule; available by prescription only. • During first three months of use, many produce symptoms similar to those of early pregnancy: nausea, breast tenderness, fluid retention. • Has been associated with such major problems as blood clots and hypertension, and also with migraines and diminished sex drive. The risks rise dramatically for smokers and for women over 35. • Possible link to increased risk of cervical cancer, gall bladder disease and benign liver tumors. • Not recommended for women who have had heart attacks or strokes, or who have diabetes or circulatory disorders; taking certain antibiotics and other prescription drugs may diminish the pill's effectiveness.
• Protects against STDs, including AIDS; may protect against cervical cancer. • Available without prescription.	• Must be applied immediately before intercourse; can result in diminished sexual sensation. • May break or slip off during the sex act. • Cannot be used by those allergic to rubber.
• Very safe. • Can be inserted up to two hours before intercourse. • May protect against some STDs.	• Increased risk of urinary tract infections; cannot be used by women allergic to rubber. • Available by prescription only; must be replaced every year or two; must be refitted after pregnancy or after significant weight gain or loss. • Spermicidal jelly or cream must be reapplied each time before engaging in intercourse. • Must be left in place for six hours after intercourse. • Requires proper washing and storing.
• Easy to use because spermicide is self-contained. • Available without prescription. • May be inserted up to 24 hours before intercourse. • May protect against some STDs.	• May be hard to remove or may shred while in place; can irritate vaginal lining. • Higher-than-average failure rate among women who have given birth. • No long-term studies have been conducted on the safety of the sponge. • Women are advised not to use the sponge while menstruating. • Must be left in place for six hours after intercourse.
• Once IUD is inserted, user is protected from unwanted pregnancy for a year.	• Must be inserted by a physician and replaced yearly. • May cause heavy bleeding and cramping during menstruation, and spotting between periods for the first few months. • Increases the risk of pelvic inflammatory disease, which can impair fertility. • Can cause perforation of the uterine wall. • Can be expelled during menstruation. • Dramatically increases the risk of miscarriage if pregnancy occurs; increases risk of ectopic pregnancy (the development of a fertilized egg in one of the fallopian tubes).
• Available without prescription. • May protect against some STDs.	• Must be applied shortly before intercourse and reapplied each time before engaging in intercourse; messy. • May cause irritation (which usually subsides if another brand is used). • No douching or bathing allowed for six to eight hours after use.

A Guide to Sexually Transmitted Diseases

DISEASE	SYMPTOMS	HEALTH EFFECTS	TREATMENT
Chlamydia (Agent: Chlamydia trachomatis bacteria)	Urinary discomfort and vaginal or penile discharge as early as 10 days or as late as several months after exposure. Often the attack is so mild that it is ignored. Many men and women are asymptomatic.	Severe infections can cause sterility in men and infertility in women. Women may suffer pelvic inflammatory disease and an increased risk of ectopic pregnancy, miscarriage, premature delivery and postpartum infections. Infected mothers can pass the disease to their infants during delivery.	Antibiotics are effective.
Genital Herpes (Agent: Herpes simplex virus)	Outbreak begins two days to three weeks after exposure with tingling or itching in the genital area or pain in the testicles in men, followed by blisters that quickly burst and become sores. Stress, menstruation and lowered resistance because of illness can trigger new outbreaks, but recurrences are almost always less severe than the initial episode. The disease may lie dormant for several years, even though the virus remains in the body.	Women with herpes are at greater risk of miscarriage and premature delivery. If the mother has active sores, she may transmit herpes to her infant during a vaginal delivery, causing blindness, brain damage, or even death. Herpes is also associated with an increased risk of cervical cancer.	The antiviral drug acyclovir (trade name Zovirax) can prevent recurrences or reduce their severity. Xylocaine cream, ethyl chloride or acyclovir in ointment form can reduce the pain from blisters and shorten the duration of the first attack.
Genital Warts (Agent: Human papillomavirus)	Appearance of warts three weeks to three months after exposure. Often undetected by women, because they can be hidden inside the vagina, genital warts are very contagious.	They tend to be more annoying than dangerous, although genital warts have been associated with an increased risk of cervical cancer in women.	Surgery or cauterization may be required, but most genital warts can be removed with a chemical or frozen with dry ice or liquid nitrogen.
Gonorrhea (Agent: Gonococcus bacteria)	Painful urination and vaginal or penile discharge two days to three weeks after exposure. Up to 60 percent of women and some men have no symptoms or only very mild symptoms. This can lead to their mistaking gonorrhea for another condition like a bladder infection.	In men, untreated gonorrhea sometimes leads to abscesses, arthritis, meningitis or other complications. In women, pelvic inflammatory disease may result if the gonorrhea spreads to the uterus and fallopian tubes, a possible cause of tubal damage and infertility. Infected mothers can pass the disease to their newborns during delivery.	Antibiotics will cure gonorrhea. Some strains are resistant to penicillin, but other antibiotics will be effective on these strains.
Syphilis (Agent: Spirochete bacteria)	A painless genital sore, or chancre, usually appearing within nine to 90 days after exposure. Because the chancre is frequently inside the vagina, 90 percent of affected women are unaware that they have it. The chancre can also be hidden in men. It usually disappears in a few weeks, but other symptoms can occur up to six months later. These include swollen lymph glands in the genital area, rashes, mouth sores, sore throat, fever, joint aches and hair loss.	In its late stages, which can occur years after exposure, syphilis can attack any organ in the body, resulting in paralysis, blindness, heart disease or insanity. Pregnant women who are not treated within the first 16 weeks after conception can infect their fetuses; babies can be stillborn, or else born with the disease or a deformity.	Penicillin and tetracycline are effective.

Healthy Sex

If you have had one sexual partner for many years, Sexually Transmitted Diseases, or STDs, are probably not something you need to worry about. But anyone who has had multiple sexual partners, or has a relationship with someone who has multiple partners, may be at risk. Though not as common as colds, STDs are among the most prevalent kinds of infections in the United States. Researchers have identified more than 20 STDs, and the most common ones — which are listed in the chart at left — affect an estimated 10 to 15 million Americans.

STDs are caused by organisms that, in most instances, enter the body through mucous membranes of the genitals, anus or mouth. Most are spread by intimate contact with an infected person. A few, like herpes and syphilis, may be transmitted nonsexually, though almost never by coming in contact with inanimate objects, since organisms that cause STDs usually die within a minute outside the body.

Self-diagnosis and treatment of STDs is never advisable. Some STDs manifest similar symptoms but require different treatments and some symptoms that appear to be STDs may actually signal different problems, like vaginitis and yeast infections. Finally, some STD symptoms vanish temporarily, but the disease is still active. It is important to consult a physician at the first sign of an infection.

Most STDs are not life-threatening, and most can be cured or at least controlled with early diagnosis. Getting prompt treatment is crucial, since some STDs, when left untreated, have caused pelvic inflammatory disease in women, which can lead to infertility. Other STDs can injure and even kill the newborn infants of infected mothers. In addition, there are links between certain STDs and cancer.

For protection against these complications, and because early diagnosis is sometimes complicated by a lack of detectable symptoms, health officials stress the importance of prevention. Obviously it is best if you can communicate openly with your partner about any exposure either of you may have had to STDs.

The best protective measures are barrier methods of birth control — condoms and diaphragms — combined with spermicides. A condom with a spermicide that contains nonoxydol-9, an ingredient found in many contraceptive jellies and foams, is highly recommended.

Avoiding AIDS

Virtually unheard of until the 1980s, the disease clinically known as Acquired Immune Deficiency Syndrome is now recognized as a worldwide epidemic. AIDS is caused by a blood-borne virus that attacks the body's immune system and ultimately renders it incapable of defending itself against infection and illness.

The AIDS virus appears to spread mainly through an exchange of bodily fluids. Transmission can occur through microscopic tears in the skin, and some recent findings indicate that, during intercourse, the virus may also be able to infect vaginal or rectal cells in unbroken skin. Sexually, the greatest risk of transmission is through anal intercourse, which can cause tears in rectal tissue. However, instances of the virus spreading through vaginal intercourse are on the rise, and the U.S. Surgeon General has stated that heterosexual persons are increasingly at risk. Still, the great majority of cases in the United States involve homosexual males and intravenous drug users who have used contaminated needles — another way that the virus can be passed. AIDS can be transmitted from an infected mother to her unborn child. Once the disease develops, it is fatal: No effective treatment has been found.

Although the risk of being infected with AIDS during the first sexual contact with an infected partner is less than one in 100, the consensus of experts is that the risk increases with each successive sexual contact. Having multiple sex partners also increases the risk of getting AIDS, and studies indicate that women are at greater risk than men: The virus is found in much higher concentrations in semen than in vaginal secretions.

The AIDS virus can be detected by a blood test, but the virus may not show up in a test for as many as three months after the date of exposure to it. Carrying the virus does not automatically indicate an active infection; however, no one knows how many AIDS carriers will become ill. People who think that they may have been exposed to AIDS should seek testing immediately.

Minimizing the risk is possible for any well-informed, sexually active person. Among the strategies recommended by health officials:

• Women should not engage in sexual intercourse with a new partner unless he is wearing a condom, preferably one treated with a spermicide that contains nonoxydol-9, which may kill the AIDS virus.

• Both men and women should get medical treatment immediately for any STD. Herpes, gonorrhea or syphilis may increase the risk of AIDS being transmitted between partners. Women should learn as much as possible about their partner's sexual history; bisexuality or intravenous drug use is cause for concern.

A Guide to the Exercises

The following chapters offer four types of exercises that are of roughly equal importance for sexual fitness. The exercises in Chapter Two are routines for toning and stretching muscles that are designed to be performed with a partner. You can use the stretching exercises as a warm-up and cool-down for the strengthening movements. As part of your warm-up, you and your partner should devote at least five minutes to performing an aerobic activity such as walking, running in place or riding an exercise bicycle. The two of you should also add an aerobic exercise to the workouts in this book — in sessions that last at least 20 minutes — since it is aerobic exercise that has been the basis for most of the studies linking sexuality to fitness.

The sensuality and relaxation exercises in Chapter Three are intended to expand the way in which you relate to your partner physically and emotionally. By focusing on various methods of touching, the routines help de-emphasize the performance aspect of sex. As exercises, they are not work, but should be done in a spirit of play.

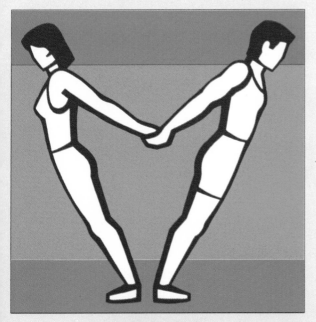

STRETCHING
pages 64-77

Partner stretches are an effective and enjoyable way to improve flexibility and ease muscular tension and stiffness. They can be performed as separate routines or as part of a warm-up or cool-down.

SHAPING AND TONING
pages 30-63

These exercises improve strength and muscular endurance, and they cover all the major muscle groups. Working with a partner allows you better to stabilize your body and also to fine-tune the resistance of each exercise.

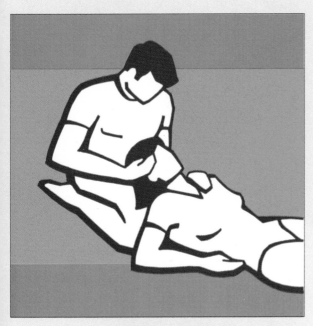

SENSUALITY
pages 82-97

Touching is the key to enhancing sensuality, and all the sequences in this section show proven techniques for awakening your skin's sensitivity. There are also stroking sequences for giving your partner a sensual massage.

BODY AWARENESS
pages 98-123

This section provides choreographed movement exercises for developing a heightened sense of how your body moves and interacts with a partner. A series of alignment exercises can expand your range of motion.

CHAPTER TWO

Working Out Together

Couples' exercises for shaping, toning and flexibility

Couples who exercise together, performing endurance activities like running and biking, often find that sharing workouts can contribute to their relationship. The activity can build mutual understanding, promote companionship and give both partners added motivation to remain committed to an exercise program. For some busy couples, their joint workout may be one of the few chances they have during the day to spend time together.

The partner exercises in this chapter offer these benefits along with additional advantages. In performing most of them, you work in tandem, and your joint participation becomes an integral part of the exercise. You help each other stretch, or provide the resistance needed for an effective muscle-strengthening and -toning routine. A shared effort to boost your overall fitness and well-being, as well as improve your appearance, will help the two of you become attuned to each other's body in a new way and reach a deeper level of intimacy — all of which can enhance your sex life.

The exercises that follow are designed to provide a complete muscle-toning routine for the legs, middle body and upper body, plus stretches for flexibility. You should supplement this workout with aerobic activity, such as running, walking or aerobic dance, three times a week for at least 30 minutes per session (including warm-up and cool-down) to build cardiovascular endurance. The muscles of the stomach, hips and thighs are especially important during the sex act, and the strengthening and toning routines on pages 30-51 will help develop these areas.

During the muscle-toning exercises on pages 30-63, your partner will rely on you to provide the proper resistance to work against. Be sure to exert even pressure to create a smooth, rhythmic motion, especially if one of you is stronger than the other, and adjust your resistance accordingly. As a rule, you should use about 50 percent of your maximum strength when pushing. Each set of exercises requires 12 to 15 repetitions, with each repetition taking four to six seconds. If it takes much longer than that, you are probably offering too much resistance — that is, one partner is pushing too hard. If the repetition takes less than four seconds, it may mean that one partner is not pushing hard enough. Both partners should regulate their effort so that they exercise at a moderate tempo. If either partner is out of shape, start with fewer than 12 repetitions per set.

In the stretches on pages 64-77, work gently and evenly. Be aware of your partner's range of motion. Help him or her to increase flexibility gradually. Do not let your partner stretch far beyond a comfortable range.

Although individual variations in strength and flexibility are enormous, in general, because of physiological differences, men are stronger than women, while women are more flexible than men. This means that a woman may have trouble with the push-ups on pages 56-57, while her partner may find it difficult to do certain stretches. Couples should take these differences into account when performing the exercises. However, men's and women's leg muscles are close to being comparable in size and strength. This means that partners should be able to supply one another with virtually equal resistance when they are performing lower body exercises.

Throughout the workout, breathe fully and rhythmically without holding your breath. When you are lying on your back, keep the small of your back on the floor to avoid back sprain. During exercises in which you are standing, keep your knees and elbows slightly bent; locking them can cause joint injuries. Whenever appropriate, each partner should perform exercises for both sides of the body. As soon as one partner finishes a given routine, the other partner should perform it.

Because these exercises afford you and your partner an opportunity to be close physically, you should make communication a priority. Be sensitive to each other, paying close attention to verbal and nonverbal cues. For example, you need to know if you are offering the right

Strengthening Your Sexual Muscles

◆ Good muscle tone throughout the body contributes to sexual expression, but you can particularly benefit from developing strength in the group known as the pubococcygeal, or PC, muscles. These muscles are located in the area known as the pelvic floor. Both men and women can benefit from pelvic floor exercises, known as Kegel exercises.

◆ You can locate your PC muscles and test their strength during urination. Contract your muscles and try to stop the flow. If you can do so easily, your PC muscles are probably well toned. If the flow continues or merely diminishes, your PC muscles are probably weak and in need of exercise.

◆ Kegel exercises for women: Contract the pelvic floor muscles for a second or two, then release them. Repeat 10 times, slowly working up to 20 sets a day. You can practice these exercises any time, sitting, standing or lying down. You can also try tightening your muscles around your partner during intercourse, which is highly pleasurable for both partners. Some women report that strengthening their PC muscles enables them to reach orgasm more easily; others say that their orgasms are more intense.

◆ Kegel exercises for men: Squeeze your PC muscles for three seconds, then release. Begin by doing 10-15 repetitions twice a day, gradually working up to 60-70 repetitions. Men have reported that the exercises give them stronger, more intense orgasms and better control over ejaculation. Also, a number of urologists report that for some of their patients, exercises have improved the functioning of their prostate gland.

amount of resistance for your partner to work against in the muscle-toning exercises or if your partner is achieving an adequate stretch without overreaching. It is a good idea to inquire repeatedly how the other person feels as you move through the routines. Ask if your partner would like you to provide more or less resistance or allow you a greater or more restricted range of motion.

To get the most benefits from the exercises in this chapter, perform a five-minute warm-up doing an exercise that uses the large muscle groups. Among the most convenient are brisk walking, running in place and jumping rope.

In addition, there is a set of internal muscles that can enhance sexual pleasure. These are the pubococcygeal, or PC, muscles, located along the floor of the pelvis. Exercises for the PC muscles in women were developed in the 1940s by gynecologist Arnold Kegel as a means of controlling the urinary stress incontinence that some women develop as a result of childbirth. These so-called Kegel exercises are often recommended for pregnant women as a way of strengthening the pelvic floor in preparation for delivery. Both men and women who regularly perform Kegel exercises often find that toning the muscles in this area can improve their sex lives *(see box above)*.

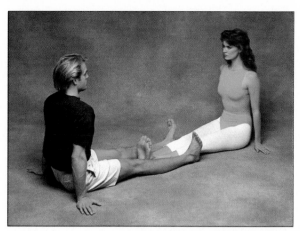

Sit on the floor facing each other, with your hands slightly behind you for balance. **SHE:** Extend your legs in front of you. **HE:** Place your feet against the outside of her calves *(above)*. Resist as she spreads her legs apart *(right)*. **SHE:** After you have opened your legs as far as is comfortable, return to the starting position, resisting while he pushes.

Lower Body/1

For most daily activities in which we use our legs, we rely on muscular endurance, the ability of a muscle to continue contracting over a long period of time. Running and walking, in particular, are dynamic endurance activities, in which muscles contract and relax repeatedly. Moreover, these upright activities call upon muscles along the back of the leg; muscles in the front are typically weaker, since they usually function to maintain balance and control, while the rear muscles propel you against gravity and friction.

The exercises here and in the following two sections are designed to help build strength along with static endurance — a muscle's ability to remain contracted for a long period of time, which is usually measured by the length of time you can hold a particular body position. Developing static endurance will give you greater stamina during lovemaking. The exercises also focus on strengthening and toning muscles along the front and side of the thighs, which are often in contact with your partner and provide support for sexual positions that involve kneeling.

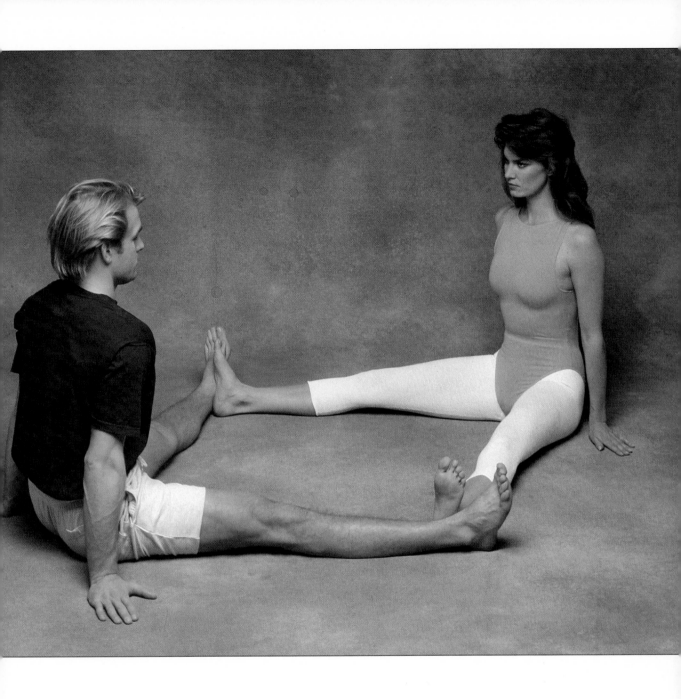

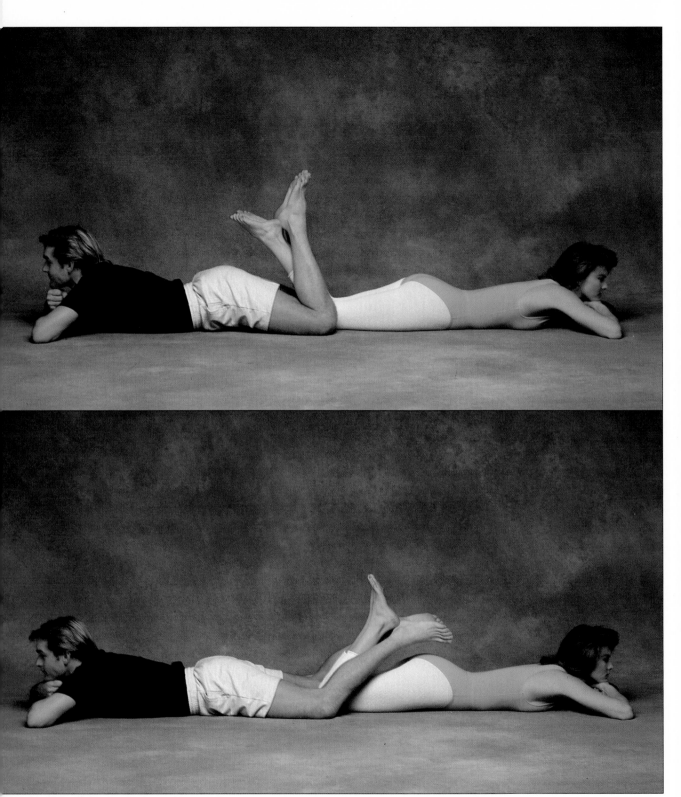

Lower Body/2

HE: Hook your feet around the outsides of her feet. Move your feet toward your buttocks while she resists *(top)*. **SHE:** Move your feet toward your buttocks while he resists *(bottom)* to return to the starting position.

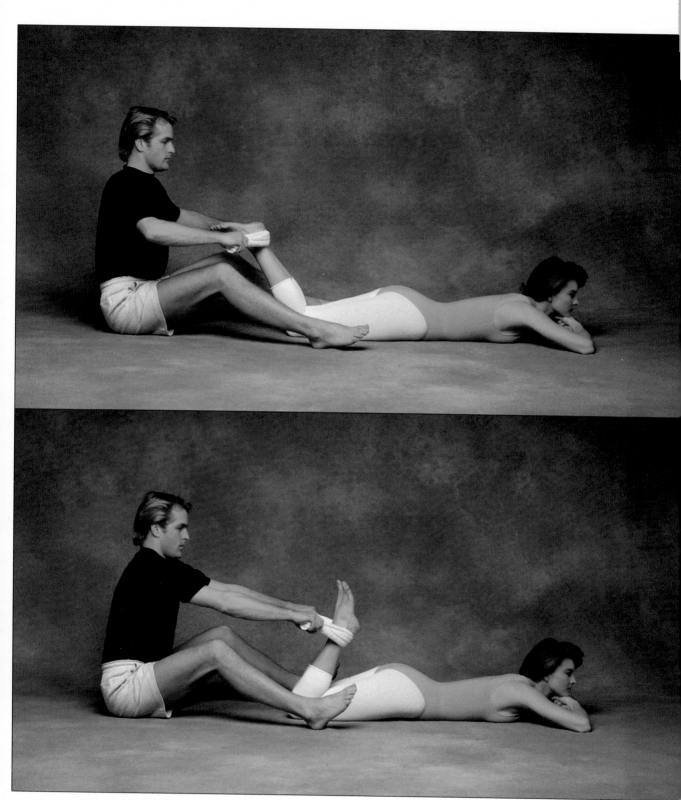

SHE: Lie on your stomach facing away from him with your legs bent at a 90-degree angle. **HE:** Wrap a towel around her ankles and hold *(top)*. **SHE:** Move your feet toward your buttocks as he resists *(bottom)*. Resist his pull to return to the first position.

Lower Body/3

SHE: Lie down with your arms straight out to the sides, your legs bent, your feet flat on the floor. **HE:** Kneel between her feet, cross your arms and place your hands on her knees *(below)*. As she resists, push her knees apart *(below right)*. Resist as she presses her knees back together.

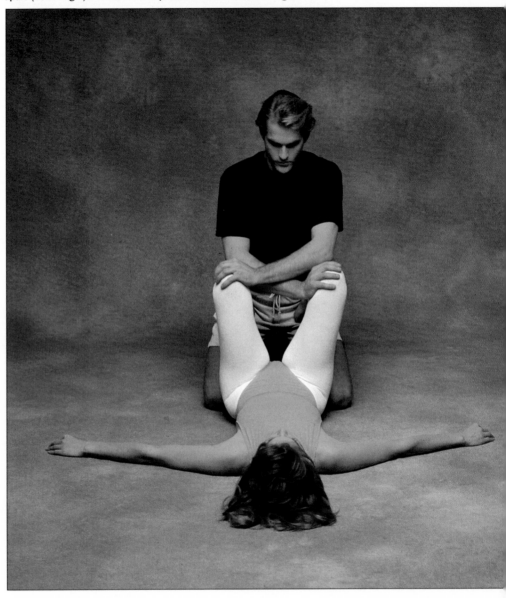

Lower Body/4

Lie on your backs with your arms at your sides and your buttocks about six inches apart. Raise your legs and bend them at the knees *(top)*. **SHE:** Place your lower legs between his and press outward. **HE:** Resist her motion *(above)*. **SHE:** Resist as he presses back to the starting position.

Stand face to face about three feet apart and hold each other's hands lightly *(right)*. Slowly lower yourselves until your upper and lower legs form 90-degree angles *(above)*. Hold for 30 seconds. Slowly rise to the standing position. Repeat this exercise two or three times. As you become stronger, gradually increase the time you hold the bent-legs position to 60 seconds.

Lie on your backs with your buttocks about six inches apart. **SHE:**
Spread your legs apart, keeping your knees straight and your feet
in the air. **HE:** Lift your legs and bend your knees so that your
lower legs rest on her inner thighs *(above)*. **BOTH:** Using your
abdominal muscles, reach toward your partner's hands, slowly
lifting your upper bodies off the floor no higher than the bottoms
of your shoulder blades *(opposite)*. Then lower yourselves.

Middle Body/1

Firming your abdomen accomplishes more than improving your posture and trimming your appearance. Strong abdominal muscles can also relieve the back of some of its burden of supporting the body. The abdominal muscles are usually much weaker than the opposing lower back muscles; therefore, the exercises on these two pages and the following 12 emphasize movements that work your abdominals, which should help pull your pelvis into better alignment and relieve stress on your back.

Although the sit-up has long been considered one of the best exercises for shaping and firming muscles in the middle body, in fact sit-ups pose some risk to the vulnerable lower back when performed with straight legs. Safer sit-ups are shown above and on pages 40-41 and 50-51. In these variations, bending your knees or lifting your legs relieves pressure on your lower back.

A partner can contribute to the effectiveness of these exercises in two ways. Since there is a propensity to jerk or lunge during abdominal work, he or she can help to stabilize you, so that your movements are smooth and continuous. In addition, you should breathe in during the relaxed phase and breathe out during the exertion. If you and your partner synchronize your breathing, you may find it easier to inhale and exhale at the proper time.

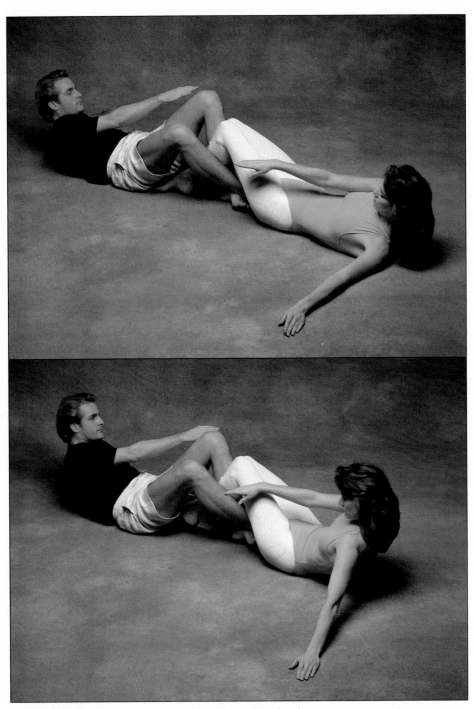

Lie on your back with your knees bent, your ankles crossed and your feet on the floor. Reach your right arms forward toward your left knees. **SHE:** Put your bent legs in between your partner's legs. Reach your right arm forward toward your left knee *(top)*. **BOTH:** Lift your right shoulders and torsos up toward your left knees *(above)*.

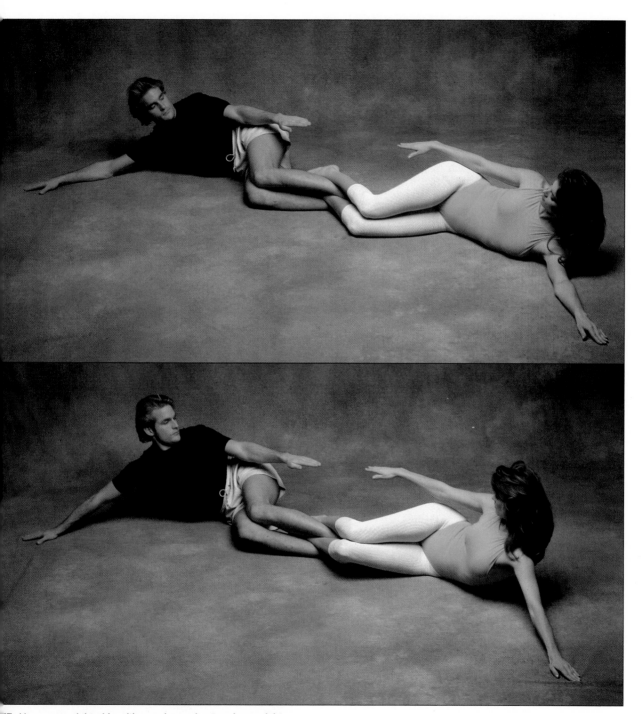

HE: Lie on your right side with your knees bent and your right arm extended. Interlock your feet with hers and extend your left arm toward her. **SHE:** Lie on your left side with your knees bent, your left arm bracing yourself, your right arm extended toward him *(top)*. **BOTH:** Lift your torsos toward each other *(above)*.

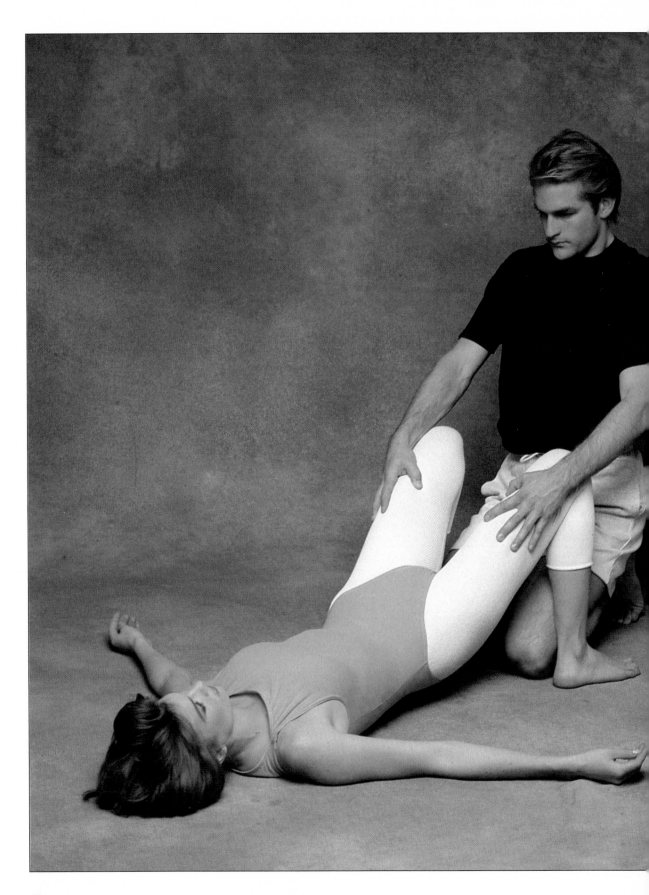

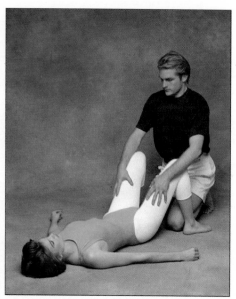

Middle Body/3

SHE: Lie on your back with your arms out to the sides, your knees bent and your feet flat on the floor. **HE:** Kneel between her legs and place your hands down on the front of her thighs and pull toward her knees *(above)*. **SHE:** Lift your hips, contracting your pelvic floor muscles and buttocks *(left)* and then lower your hips.

Middle Body/4

Stand with your hands on your hips and your knees straight or slightly flexed *(top right)*. Tuck in your abdomen while tipping your hips up *(bottom right)*. Return to the starting position.

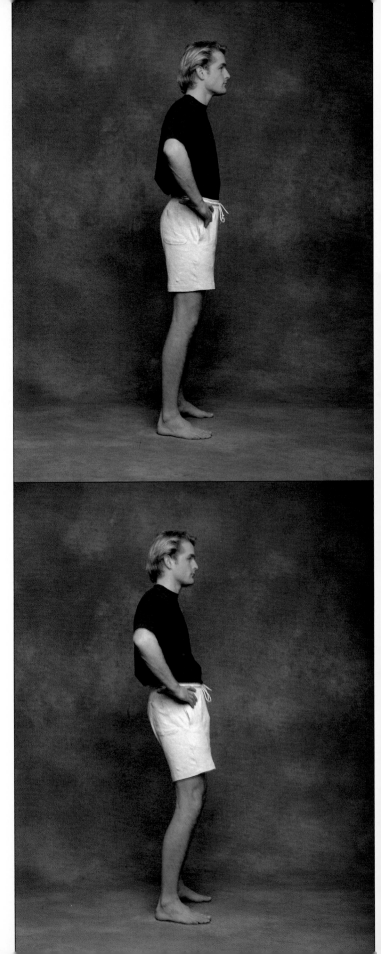

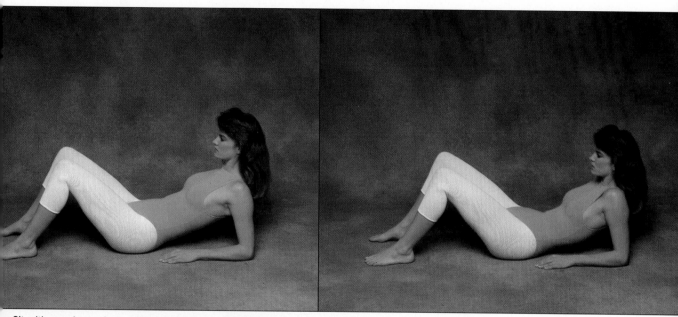

Sit with your knees bent and your feet flat on the floor. Lean back, resting on your forearms (above). Slowly round your lower back toward the floor (right). Return to the starting position.

Middle Body/5

Lie on your backs head to head, with your feet in the air, your knees slightly bent and your ankles crossed. Keeping your elbows bent, hold each other's upper arms *(opposite)*. Contract your abdominals and lift your hips off the floor *(above)*. Slowly lower your hips.

Lie on your backs, head to head. Bend your arms above you and hold each other's forearms, your legs at a right angle. Keeping your knees together and your abdominals contracted, slowly lower your legs to the left until they are on the floor *(left)*. Lift your knees and bring them back toward your chests *(below)*. Repeat to the other side *(below right)*.

Middle Body/7

SHE: Kneel facing him with your legs spread comfortably apart. **HE:** Sit with your legs between hers, your knees bent and your feet flat on the floor. Curve your back slightly and cross your arms in front of your chest. **SHE:** Cross your hands over each other and place them on his crossed arms *(right)*. Push him down. **HE:** Resist her push as you lower yourself slowly *(below right)*. Return to the starting position.

Lie on your backs facing each other and your arms extended toward your partner. **SHE:** Bend your knees and cross your ankles, keeping your feet flat on the floor. **HE:** Bend your knees and cross your ankles around and under her legs *(opposite top)*. **BOTH:** Contract your abdominal muscles to lift your upper torsos off the floor as you reach toward each other *(opposite bottom)*.

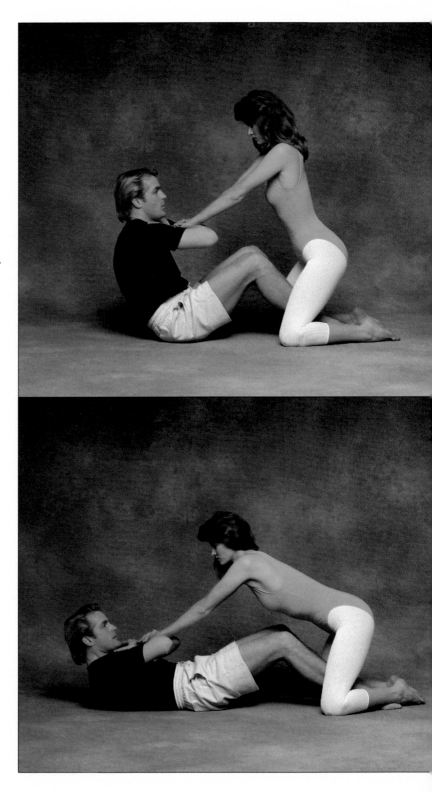

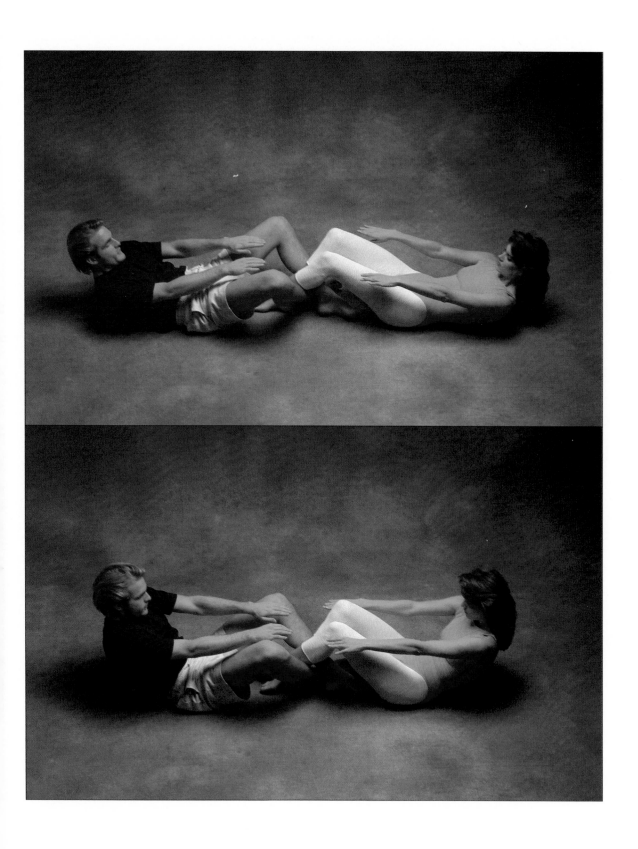

Upper Body/1

In most people, the muscles of the arms and shoulders are the least used muscles of the body; yet they are often called into play during sex for raising and lowering yourself, and for supporting your upper body. A typical — and excellent — exercise for conditioning these muscles is the classic push-up. But the push-up and many other solo strengthening exercises that do not utilize weights rely on your own body weight to supply the resistance — and many people do not have the upper body strength to lift their own body weight even once.

By working with a partner, however, you can adjust the resistance of an exercise to your strength level, enabling you to execute the proper number of repetitions with an adequate work load. One of the best ways to achieve this is by using a towel, which can function much like a dumbbell or a wall pulley, as in the exercises on pages 54-55 and 58-59. It can also assist you in performing the push-ups on pages 56-57.

When performing the exercises, the person applying resistance should take care not to overpower the more active partner. Largely because of genetic factors, a male partner is likely to have stronger, larger upper body muscles than a female, and men therefore may have to use only about half of their maximum strength to provide smooth, even resistance during the exercises. Similarly, when a man is the active partner, he may have to work at less than his maximum effort. But the exercises are designed so that either partner can supply enough resistance, and adjust that resistance, for improvements in strength and muscle tone to occur.

Sit with the soles of your feet pressed together and your knees bent. **HE:** Hold the middle of a rolled towel with an overhand grip while she holds the ends. **SHE:** Pull the towel toward you while he resists *(above left)*. **HE:** Pull the towel back toward you while she resists *(above)*.

Upper Body/2

HE: Lie on your back with your knees bent and your feet flat on the floor. Grip the ends of two rolled towels overhand. With your elbows bent, raise your arms. **SHE:** Stand straddling his hips and cross the ends of the towels in front of you *(above)*. Pull the towels apart until his wrists are crossed while he resists *(above right)*. **HE:** Pull your arms sideways and down while she resists.

SHE: Sit with your knees bent and the soles of your feet together. Bend your arms at your sides and hold the ends of a rolled towel. **HE:** Stand behind her and grip the center of the towel overhand *(below)*. Lift the towel to chest height while she resists *(left)*. **SHE:** Pull out and down while he resists until you reach the starting position.

Upper Body/3

SHE: Assume the standard push-up position. **HE:** Straddle her at her thighs, keeping your knees bent. Support her hips with a folded towel *(opposite)*. **SHE:** Lower yourself slowly to within an inch or two of the floor while he helps to support you *(above)*, then raise yourself up.

Upper Body/4

HE: Sit with your legs crossed and your knees raised. Hold the middle of a rolled towel in front of you with your arms forming right angles. **SHE:** Stand facing him. Hold the ends of the towel in an underhand grip with your arms at your sides *(above)*. Pull the towel by curling your hands toward your shoulders; avoid moving your upper arms *(above right)* while he resists. **HE:** Pull the towel back down while she resists.

Stand up with your feet about shoulder-width apart and about one foot from each other. **SHE:** Hold the middle of a rolled towel in your left hand. With your arms above your head, bend your right arm to support your left elbow as you dangle the towel behind you. **HE:** Standing behind her, hold the ends of the towel in front of you with your elbows bent *(below)*. **SHE:** Raise your left forearm as he resists *(right)*. Return to the starting position.

Stand about one foot apart with your legs about shoulder-width
apart. **SHE:** Hold your elbows in front of you at chest level.
HE: Stand behind her and place your hands behind her elbows
(above). **SHE:** Push your elbows out to the sides while he resists
(above right). **HE:** Push her arms back to the starting position as
she resists.

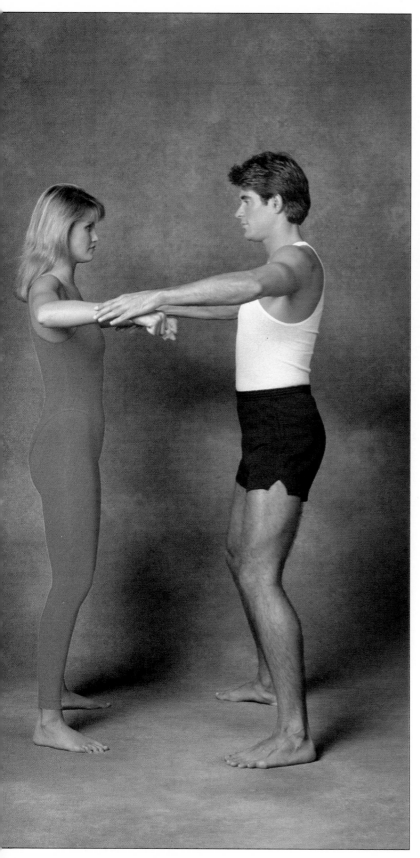

Stand facing each other. **SHE:** With your elbows bent out to your sides at a 90-degree angle, hold your forearms in front of you at chest level. **HE:** With your arms at chest level and your elbows bent, rest your hands on her forearms *(left)*. Push downward while she resists until your hands are at waist level *(above)*. **SHE:** Push upward while he resists to resume the starting position.

Kneel facing each other and sit on your heels. Hold your arms
out in front of each other, with your elbows flexed slightly. **SHE:**
Hold your wrists together. **HE:** Place your hands on the outside
of her wrists *(opposite)*. **SHE:** Push your arms out until they are
shoulder-width apart while he resists *(above)*. **HE:** Push her
arms back to the starting position as she resists.

Partner Stretching/1

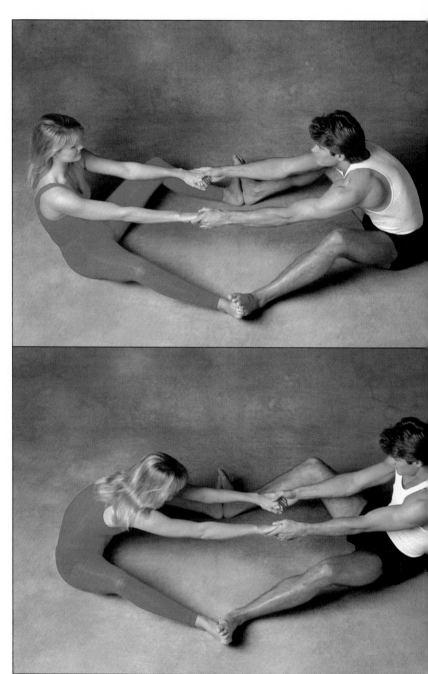

Exercising with a partner is especially beneficial for developing flexibility. By having a partner assist in a stretch, you can increase your range of motion farther than you can when the force of the stretch is provided only by your own body weight. A partner can apply more tension to your muscles, increasing the intensity and duration of a stretch.

The following pages offer a variety of static stretches — slow, deliberate movements in which you extend a muscle just beyond its normal length and hold it in that position. You should not bounce or lunge to achieve the stretch, since this can invoke a reflex in which the muscle actually contracts; instead, move gently and smoothly into the stretch. The two of you can then become sensitive to one another's level of flexibility and learn how far to stretch a particular muscle. During a stretch, muscles should feel tight but never painful. After a stretch, you should experience a pleasant release of muscular tension. Be sure to exhale as you stretch.

Hold each stretch for 15 to 30 seconds, pause, then repeat the stretch. For particularly stiff muscle groups, perform the stretch a third time. Work slowly — you will get more benefit from the stretches and they will also be more enjoyable.

Sit facing each other with your knees slightly flexed and the soles of your feet touching. Reach straight ahead and clasp hands *(top left)*. Lean over in the same direction *(top right)*. **BOTH:** Continue to roll in a circle: **HE:** Move backward as she moves forward *(bottom left)*. **SHE:** Move to your right as he moves to his left *(bottom right)*.

Partner
Stretching/2

Sit facing each other. Hold each other's hands and spread your legs apart. **HE:** Put your feet on her ankles *(left)*. Raise your left arm and drop your right arm to bend to the right, as she raises her right arm and drops her left *(opposite)*. **SHE:** Stretch the other way by dropping your right arm and raising your left, while he drops his left arm and raises his right *(above)*.

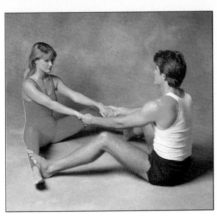

Partner
Stretching/3

Sit facing each other toe to toe, heels down, with your knees
bent. Hold hands. **BOTH:** Pull back lightly and hold *(above)*.

Kneel on the floor on all fours, with your
arms straight and your bodies parallel to
each other. Stretch your hips to the right
and hold *(opposite top)*. Then stretch to
your left and hold *(opposite bottom)*.

69

Sit back to back with your legs spread comfortably and your arms out to your sides and intertwined *(opposite).* **SHE:** Lean forward while he leans back as far as is comfortable *(above).* **HE:** Lean forward while she leans back.

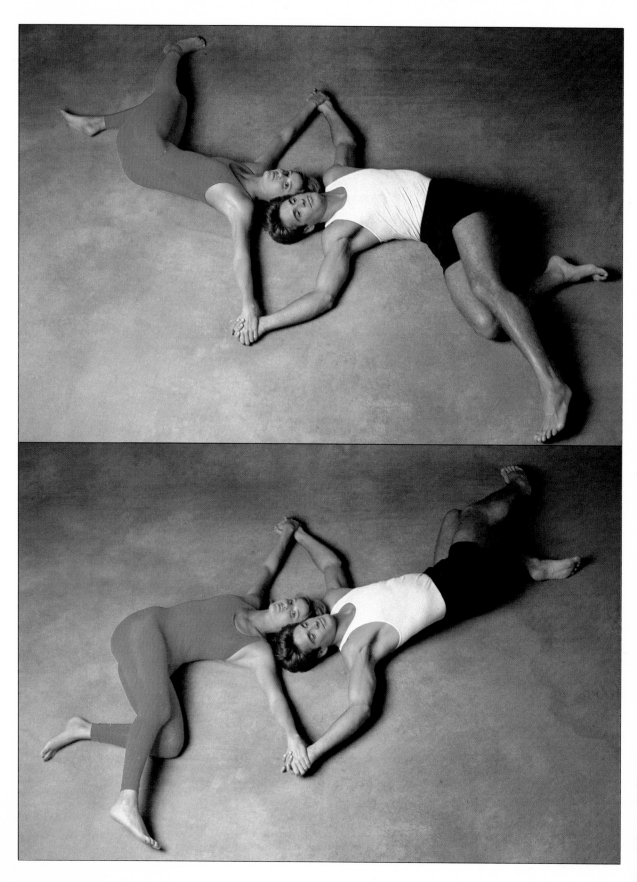

Partner Stretching/5

Lie on the floor head to head, with your left ears touching and your arms outstretched. Hold hands. Twist, bringing your bent right knees to the floor and keeping your left legs straight *(opposite top)*. Hold. Bring your knees to the other side, bending your left legs and straightening your right ones *(opposite bottom)*.

Stand facing each other at arms' length. **HE:** Hold her left hand in your right hand and hold your left foot behind you in your left hand. **SHE:** Hold his right hand in your left and hold your right foot behind you in your right hand *(below)*. Hold. Change hands and feet. Repeat.

Partner Stretching/6

HE: Sit on the floor with your legs extended in front of you. Reach out to hold her wrists. **SHE:** Stand in front of him with your feet against his and hold his wrists. Lean backward and hold *(above)*. **BOTH:** Reverse positions and hold *(opposite)*.

Partner
Stretching/7

Stand side by side with your legs spread comfortably apart. **SHE:** With your left foot against his right foot and your left arm at your side, hold the end of a folded towel in your upraised right arm. **HE:** Hold the other end of the towel in your right hand. **BOTH:** Bend to your left bringing your right arms and the towel over your heads *(left).* Stretch the other way, bringing the towel to the right and slightly in front of you *(below).*

Stand with your feet together, side by side, about three feet apart. **HE:** Bend your right arm and place your hand behind your head, lifting your elbow. **SHE:** Bend your left arm and place your hand behind your neck, lifting your elbow to touch his. Lean toward each other *(right)*. Hold. Trade places and repeat.

Stand back to back about a foot apart. Keeping your arms straight, reach behind yourselves and hold each other's wrists. Lean forward as far as you comfortably can *(right)*. Hold.

CHAPTER THREE

Sensuality

*Enhancing intimacy through
techniques of touch*

Considering that the sense of touch is so fundamental to our sense of self and so essential to emotional intimacy, it is unfortunate that adults often deprive themselves of meaningful touching. Although the sense of touch is a powerful component of human sexuality, there are many ways to touch and be touched that are sensual but not directly sexual. Learning such touching techniques can add vitality to your sex life. The exercises in this chapter are united by a common thread: They are all centered around developing the ways in which you touch your partner.

Touch is the first of the five senses to develop in the human embryo. Studies prove that touching in the form of cuddling, kissing and hugging is crucial to the physical and emotional development of the child, and babies deprived of this kind of stimulation for prolonged periods languish and fail to grow normally; some even die. Yet once a person has passed through childhood, tactile communication outside of sex may be limited to pats on the back, handshakes and the like.

The vehicle for touch is, of course, the skin, the body's largest organ system by far. Because such an enormous number of sensory receptors are embedded in the skin, it is sometimes described as an external nervous system. Certain areas of the skin are more sensitive to touch than others, and research on tactile stimulation has turned up surprising data on this variability. For example, the tip of the tongue, the fingertips and the tip of the nose are the most acutely touch-sensitive parts of the body, in that order. The face, palms of the hands and soles of the feet are also highly sensitive. Despite differences in sensitivity, though, the whole body can be viewed as an erogenous zone, as Sigmund Freud pointed out.

A sexual relationship is one of the few situations where adults can touch and be touched without restraint; even so, many lovers restrict themselves to a limited repertoire of touching. This chapter illustrates exercises that you and your partner can enjoy as pleasurable sensual experiences in and of themselves to add intimacy and variety to your sexual relationship. It also provides techniques for reducing stress and promoting relaxation. It concludes with a group of exercises derived from Yoga and from disciplines that enhance movement.

The exercises on pages 82-97 demonstrate ways to explore the erotic potential of the skin by experimenting with many different ways of being touched and touching, using the hair, the nose, the hands — and even feathers. These techniques can be used as a prelude to sexual intercourse, but they do not have to be. In fact, sex therapists use such techniques as a way of promoting closeness and trust, and affording couples an opportunity to explore physical intimacy in ways other than the strictly sexual.

For some couples, this can be reassuring. Many psychologists and sex therapists have observed that a preoccupation with intercourse as the only means of expressing intimacy and love can sometimes lead to performance anxieties that interfere with sexual pleasure. Because of this, the pioneering sex researchers Dr. William Masters and Virginia Johnson based their program for treating male and female sexual dysfunction around what they called sensate-focus exercises — explorations in intimate touching intended to be an end in themselves, not a prelude to intercourse. The aim was twofold: to put partners in tune with their own bodies and with each other's, and to teach them to give and receive pleasurable stimulation without any pressure to perform. The exercises that follow were not designed as therapy — anyone experiencing sexual difficulties should consult a trained sex therapist or physician. But like Masters and Johnson's sensate focusing, they can provide a new way for couples to interact intimately that can be removed from the sex act itself.

Besides the performance anxiety that can inhibit sexual expression, ordinary stress-related tension can affect your enjoyment of sex, too. Stress caused by your job, chores, family or any other part of your daily existence can create a mental and physical state that interferes with sexual arousal. Marriage counselors report that, along with per-

Focusing Your Mind

Sensuality starts with the ability to focus your attention on your body and on your physical relationship with your partner. If you are not mentally relaxed — if your mind is caught up with daily stresses and tensions — you may find it difficult to concentrate. The routine that follows can lead you into a pleasurable state that will help you attain the calm alertness appropriate for the exercises that follow.

1. Sit or lie down comfortably. If you are sitting, look straight ahead of you; if you are lying down, look directly at the ceiling.

2. Keeping your eyes open, look upward slowly without straining, moving only your eyes. Imagine that you can see through the top of your head. Now, still looking up, slowly close your eyelids.

3. Keep your eyes closed and focused upward, and inhale deeply through your nose. Your mouth should be closed. Hold your breath for as long as you feel comfortable, then exhale gently through your mouth, keeping your lips open only a little. As you breathe out, without opening your eyes, bring them back down slowly to the starting position.

4. Still keeping your eyes closed, breathe normally and imagine that your body is sinking deeply. You will begin to feel a pleasant floating sensation coupled with a calm alertness. Maintain this relaxed state as long as you like.

5. When you feel ready, take a deep breath through your nose, hold your breath for a moment, then exhale slowly through your slightly opened mouth. As you exhale, gradually open your eyes.

formance anxiety, stress is a major factor in some sexual dysfunction, notably inhibited sexual desire. A common signal of stress is muscular tension in the neck, shoulders and face. The partnered relaxation exercises on pages 98-103 are designed to relieve such tension.

Stress-related muscular tension may also result in tightness throughout the body, affecting proper physical alignment. This problem is addressed in the pelvic-alignment manipulations shown on pages 104-109. In the touching series on pages 110-113, you and your partner should take turns being giver and receiver, alternating active and passive roles within a session, or from one session to the next.

Prepare for these exercises by finding a room where you will not be interrupted for a certain time period, perhaps 45 minutes or more. Once you have allowed yourselves this physical privacy, try to distance yourselves mentally from cares and responsibilities. You should try to approach all the exercises in this chapter with a sense of playfulness and exploration. In general, you do not have to perform the routines in a specific order; nor do you have to do all the exercises. You can choose among them, experimenting to find out what most pleases you and your partner. When stroking, touching and caressing, avoid stressful postures.

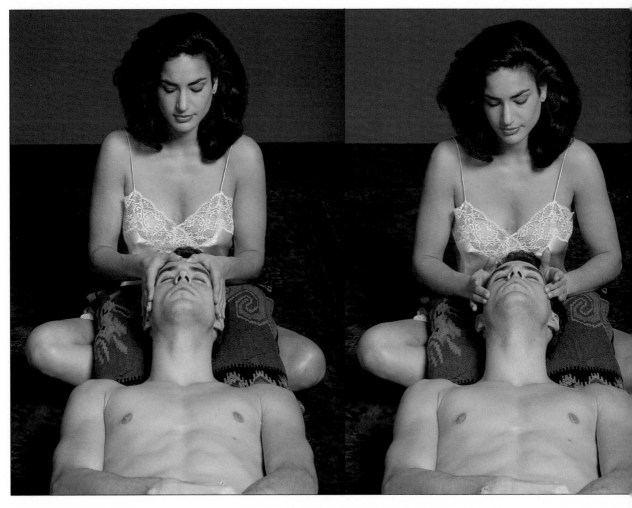

Touching/1

Although touching your partner is a natural way of expressing feeling about him or her, it can also be an avenue to becoming aware of your own sensations. The exercises on these two pages and the following four can help to focus your attention on neglected aspects of your sense of touch. They also demonstrate ways to touch your partner on the eyelids, lips and ears — areas that you may ordinarily neglect.

In order to stimulate your tactile awareness, you should pay less attention to how your partner feels than to how you feel. Consider the pleasure and new sensations you feel; this change of focus may enhance the experience for each partner.

Both of you should wear little or no clothing to increase the exposed skin surface. You can use oil or cream to reduce friction and smooth your strokes, and increase the softness of your touching.

As you and your partner become more familiar with these exercises, describe to each other the sensations they evoke. Your description should include what you like and do not like about being touched, as well as how different parts of your body react. Do not be alarmed if something that feels pleasant to you or your partner one day feels less pleasant the next day. Like the other senses, your sense of touch can encompass almost infinite variations.

Starting on your partner's forehead, slowly touch his face with both hands *(far left)*, working your way down and including the side of his face and cheeks *(second from left)*, his eyes *(third from left)* and nose *(above)*.

Touching/2

Cup both hands around the back of your partner's head, your fingertips behind her ears and your thumbs near her forehead. With short, soft movements, rub the back of her head *(left)*, then move to the front of her head *(below left)*.

Gently run your index finger over your partner's lips, paying particular attention to the outer edges.

Place one hand on your partner's forehead while keeping the other hand on top of his head. Without moving your hands, focus your attention on how his skin and hair feel to you *(right)*.

With one hand resting gently on your partner's neck or shoulder, explore one of his ears with the other hand, paying particular attention to the sensitive outer perimeter *(far right)*.

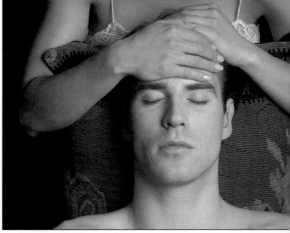

Touching/3

While your partner lies comfortably with his upper body supported by a pillow, gently rub the length of his neck with both hands *(left)*.

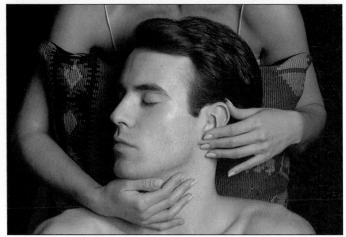

Stroking/1

Support your partner's arm with a pillow or place it in your lap. Stroke her upper arm with your thumb in a circular motion, using firm pressure.

The touching shown on these two pages and the following four involve a form of stimulation derived from massage techniques called stroking — a kind of touching that requires firm pressure to be effective. The strokes used here should be restricted to the arms, legs and trunk, avoiding delicate neck and face areas. You may want to start on your partner's arms and hands, as shown on these two pages, because they are easy to manipulate. Afterward, you can stroke your partner's lower body.

Let your partner's reactions guide you, ask which strokes are the most relaxing and pleasant. Some people like strong, circular motions with the thumb or the entire hand, while others may find such techniques too powerful. If your partner prefers, you can try a softer, gliding stroke using your fingertips.

As you stroke, change the position of your hands periodically, as shown on pages 90-93. Different hand positions will produce different sensations. Be sure that one hand touches your partner at all times. If you lift both hands simultaneously, you will break the soothing rhythm of the strokes, and your partner may feel abandoned in the middle of a pleasurable experience. Do not use direct pressure on the spine.

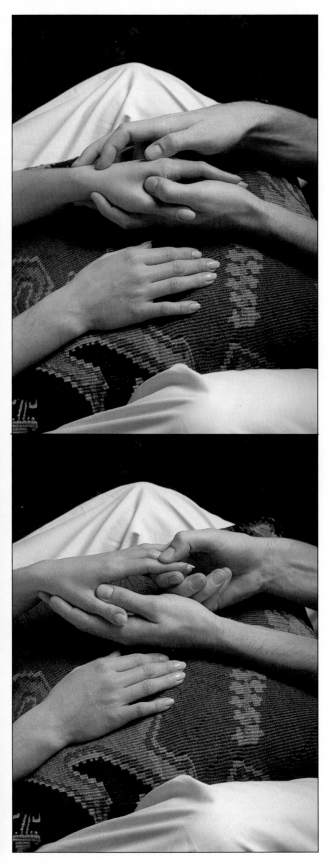

Take one of your partner's hands in yours. Probing gently, massage the back of her hand with your fingertips *(left)*. Starting at the knuckles, massage each finger to the tip and back, pressing with your thumb and index finger *(below left)*.

Stroking/2

With your partner lying on her stomach, kneel so that you are straddling her back. Keep your weight on your knees so that both of you are comfortable. Using the knuckles of both hands, stroke your partner's back along each side of her spine *(opposite)*. Place one hand on top of the other. Beginning at the base of your partner's neck, slide your hands down the length of her back *(left)*. Place both hands on your partner's shoulders *(center)*. Stroke her along the sides of her back, moving your hands down over her shoulder blades. Cross your hands and stroke your partner's back using a swirling motion toward and then away from her spine *(below)*.

Stroking/3

Kneeling next to your partner, who is lying on his back, place both your hands on his stomach. Then simultaneously stroke along his sides *(right)*. Make slow, circular motions with the fingertips of your left hand while your right hand comes down the length of his stomach *(below left)*. Cross your hands and place them on his chest. Slide both of them down the length of his stomach *(below center)*. Interweaving the fingers of both hands, slowly draw your hands down from his chest to his stomach *(below right)*.

Caressing/1

Stand facing your partner. Caress each other, nose to nose. Do not make contact with any other part of your bodies.

Most of the touching you are accustomed to involves the palms of your hands and the tips of your fingers. By using caresses — a gentle, feathery kind of touching — to explore your partner's skin with your nose, cheeks, hair and soft objects, for example, you can expand your sensitivity to different kinds of textures and varieties of tactile sensation.

When touching your partner during the exercises shown on these two pages, make sure that only one part of your body makes contact. Resist the urge to hug or hold your partner as you rub noses, as you caress her with your nose or as she rubs you with her cheek. Extraneous contact will only distract you from the main focus of these caresses.

Be creative: Do not limit your tactile experiences to the parts of the body shown here and do not limit your soft caresses to feathers and hair *(pages 96-97)*. Any suitable, soft object will do, as long as it serves to expand your awareness of the different experiences available to your skin and increases your pleasure.

Stand side by side. Starting at your partner's shoulder, caress
your partner's upper body with your nose *(top)*.

Rub your cheek along your partner's shoulders and neck *(above)*,
taking care not to touch him with any other part of your body.

Caressing/2

Have your partner recline comfortably,
leaning on his elbows with a pillow
beneath his lower back. With a feather or
other soft object, explore your partner's
body. Use soft, fluttery strokes to create
various sensations *(above)*. Using your
hair only, caress the entire length of your
partner's body *(right)*.

Relaxation/1

Discussing your feelings with another person, as you have done throughout this chapter and the previous one, can help alleviate anxiety and foster a relaxed state. By listening closely and watching, you can also learn what body positions indicate that you or your partner are tense, as well as help you identify areas of greatest muscular contraction.

One of the best ways to begin relaxing is to focus on your breathing. Most of the time, you probably pay little attention to your inhaling and exhaling: Breathing reflexes control your breathing patterns. But when you concentrate on relaxation in performing exercises like the one on this page, you should make a conscious effort to breathe slowly and deeply, maintaining a steady rhythm.

As you and your partner perform the exercises on these pages and the two following, breathe in unison, inhaling through your nose and exhaling through your mouth.

Being able to concentrate is a prerequisite to relaxation. Instead of simply pulling in air, you should con-

centrate on the expansion and widening of your chest and lungs as you breathe in. To enhance your feeling of relaxation, think of your breaths as waves that break over you, rather than as the muscular movement of your diaphragm.

Another effective method for promoting relaxation is alternately to tense and relax muscles throughout your body. The exercise on pages 100-101, in which you first contract and then relax the musculature of your face, is such an exercise, known as progressive relaxation.

Sit on the floor facing your partner and press the palms of your hands together *(opposite)*. Focus on your breathing, trying to slow yourself down and synchronize your patterns. Keep your wrists, elbows and shoulders relaxed.

Sit back to back with your elbows intertwined *(above)*. Concentrate on feeling your own breathing pattern and that of your partner. Synchronize your patterns in this position also. Although you may feel a gentle stretch in your shoulders, do not pull on your partner's arms.

Relaxation/2

Lie down next to your partner, heads side by side and feet in opposite directions, your right ears touching. Squeeze the muscles of your face together, imagining that your face is becoming narrower *(left)*. Release the muscles of your face and smile, trying to make your face as wide as possible *(above)*.

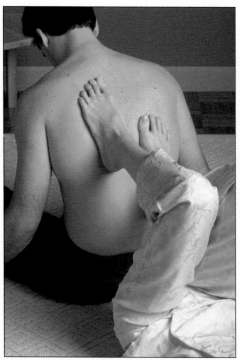

Relaxation/3

Lie on your back behind your seated
partner. Place your feet on his upper
back. Use the heels and balls of your
feet to apply pressure to his upper back,
avoiding direct pressure on the spine
(left). Slide your feet down your partner's
back in a shuffling motion *(above)*. Finish
by pressing your feet against your
partner's lower back *(right)*.

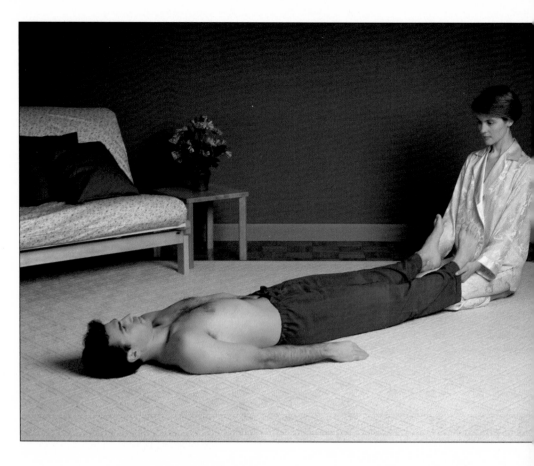

Alignment/1

Many people respond to stress by tensing their stomach and back muscles. Over time, this habitual tension creates stiffness in the hip and pelvic area, and decreases the range of motion of the joints, which may mean less flexibility and more stiffness. The exercises shown on these two pages and on pages 106-107 show how to loosen the lower back and pelvic areas by gentle manipulation that helps to realign the hips.

As.your partner consciously relaxes the muscles of his lower body, hold his feet. Keeping his legs straight, rotate his feet, gently rocking his entire leg, as shown on these two pages. By combining gentle pulling with sideways motions, you can unlock his hip joints, allowing them to move freely and without

tension. Another way of freeing the pelvis to improve alignment, shown on pages 107-108, involves lifting and lowering your partner's hips.

When you relax the muscles in the neck area, muscles elsewhere may benefit simultaneously. The head alignment exercise on pages 110-111 and the shoulder manipulations on pages 112-113 will also improve your partner's pelvic flexibility and alleviate upper body tension.

While your partner lies on his back, kneel at his feet. Grasp both his feet by the ankles, lift them and rock them gently from side to side *(above left)*. Rotate one foot at a time sideways and outward *(above right)*. Moving both feet together, lower them and rotate them inward carefully *(right)*.

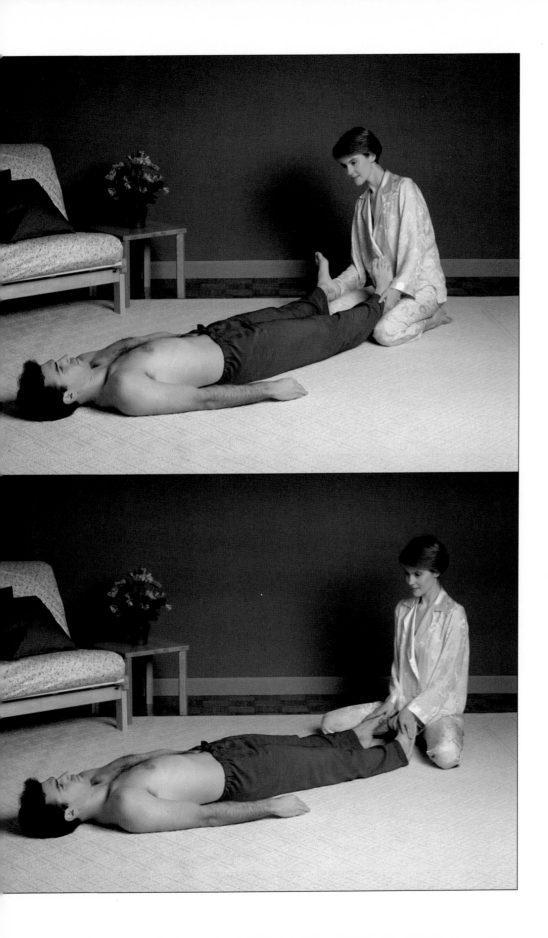

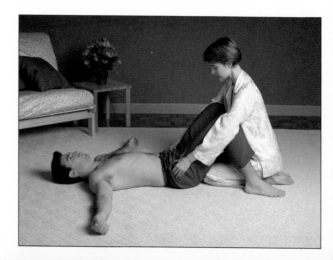

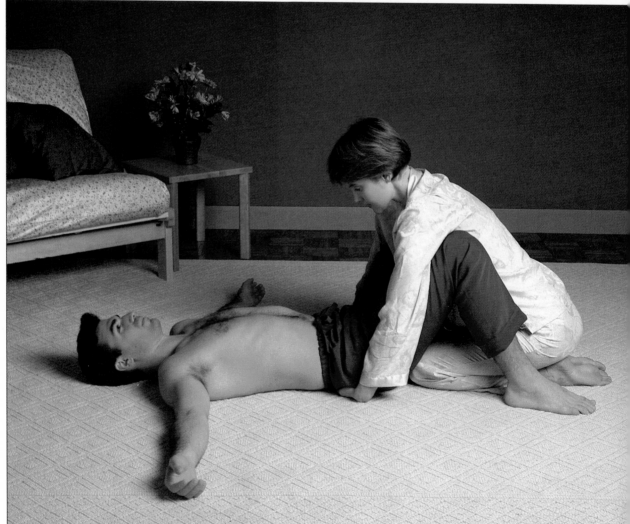

Alignment/2

Kneel between your partner's upraised knees, resting your hands on his hips *(left)*. Lift your partner's hips, slide your hands under them and keep them there for a few seconds *(below left)*. Gently ease your hands free and shift positions so that you are beside him. Kneeling at his hips, push gently on his hipbones for several seconds to relax the pelvic muscles *(below)*.

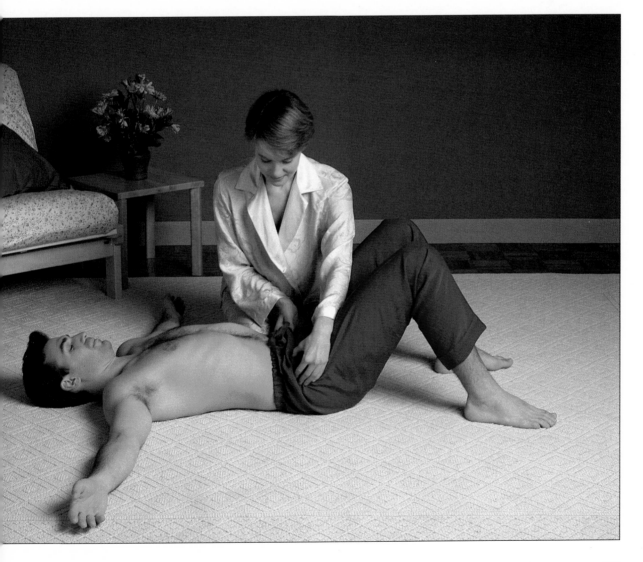

Alignment/3

With one foot in front of the other and your knees flexed, stand in front of your partner, who is lying on her back, her hands at her sides, palms facing down. Grasp her ankles and lift her, raising her hips off the floor slightly *(far left)*. She should keep her legs straight as you continue lifting, gradually raising her back off the floor *(above left)*. When only her shoulders and upper back still touch the floor, steady her momentarily *(below left)*. Slowly lower her back down.

Alignment/4

While your partner lies on her back, kneel at her head, cupping it in one hand. Gently rotate her head from side to side *(right and center).* Place your fingertips at the top of her neck and, pressing firmly, massage the base of her skull and neck, taking care to avoid direct pressure on the spine *(far right).*

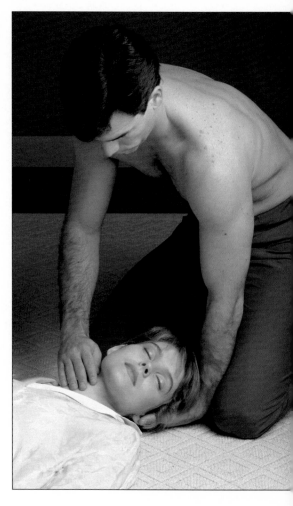

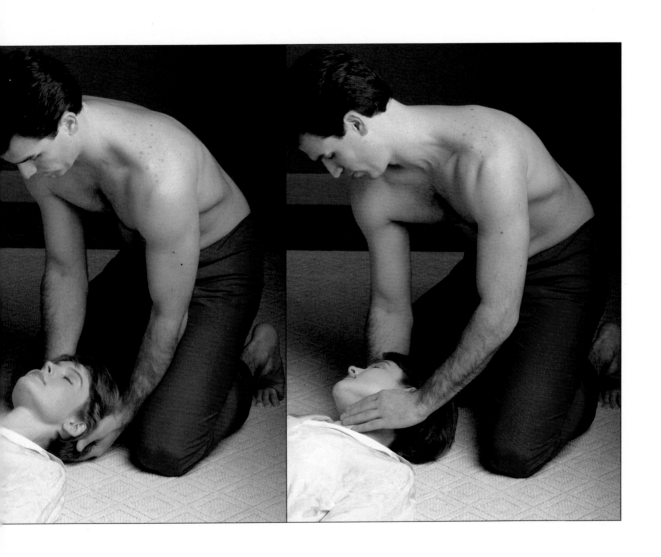

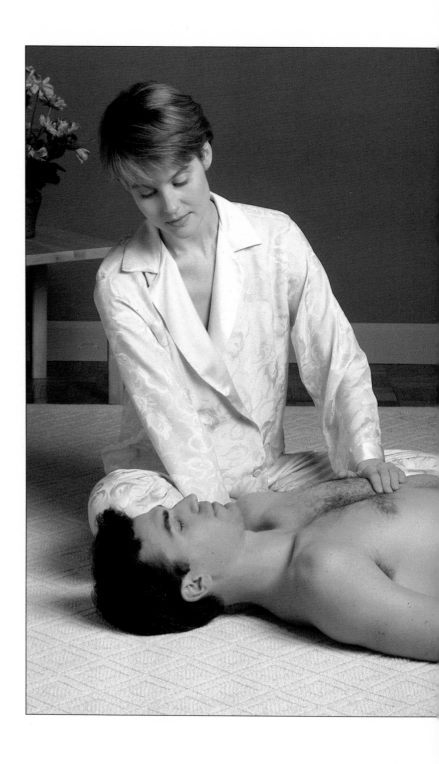

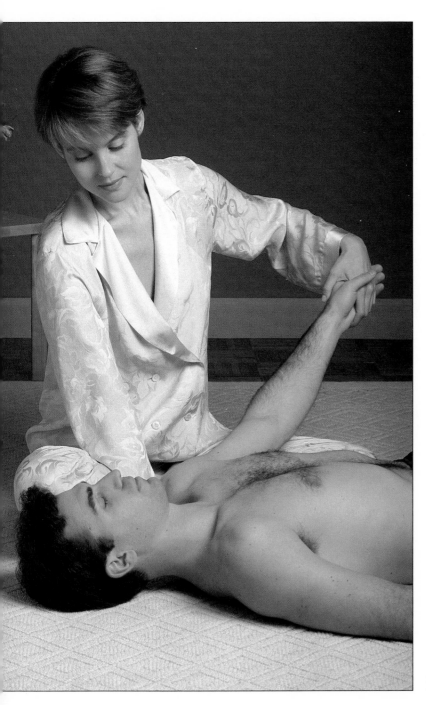

Alignment/5

While your partner lies on his back, sit
cross-legged at his left shoulder and
place one hand on his chest, the other
under his shoulder blade, pulling gently
outward with your bottom hand *(opposite)*.
Keeping this hand under his shoulder
blade, with your other hand, lift his arm,
swing it upward slowly and then pull
gently to stretch it out *(left)*.

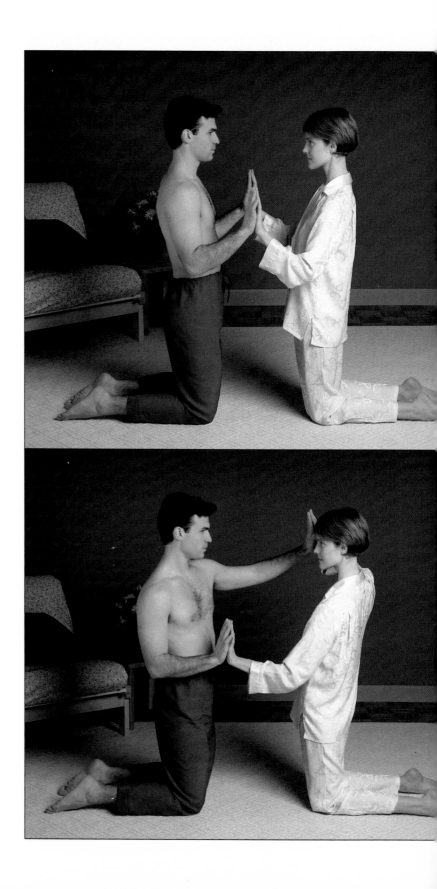

Movement/1

The exercises on these two pages and the following eight are variations on dance movements that are designed to improve your sensitivity to the way you and partner move together. Like dances, these exercises have certain patterns but still allow for creativity and improvisation. Your bodies should move together in a smooth and flowing rhythm.

It is also important that you perform these exercises in ways that allow you both to feel comfortable. For example, when pushing against each other's hands, as shown here, or against each other's legs, do not force your partner's body into the position you desire. Talk about what you are doing, focusing your attention on how you can minimize your differences in size, strength and flexibility. If, for example, a disparity in body sizes makes it difficult to perform the foot-touching exercise on pages 116-117, try positioning yourselves farther apart, even if doing so does not allow you to hold hands. Feel free to make changes in the movements to accommodate your own particular needs and take your time.

You can take turns leading these movements if you wish, but neither partner should lead all the time.

Kneel on the floor facing each other. Bend your arms and place your hands together (opposite). **Push alternately back and forth, varying the height of your arms** (below left) **and the distance between your hands and your bodies** (below right).

Movement/2

Lie on the floor, buttocks to buttocks. Lift your legs and hold hands. Touch the soles of your feet to your partner's. Push back and forth, alternating legs, up and down, in a comfortable rhythm *(opposite and above)*. Keep the muscles of your lower back and shoulders relaxed.

Movement/3

Lie on your left side on the floor with your partner on her left side behind you, her right arm around your shoulder and chest and her left arm under your neck *(near right)*. Together roll to your right, bringing your right legs to the floor, lifting your left legs toward the ceiling to propel you and holding your partner's left hand *(center)*. Keep rolling until you are lying on your right sides. Cradle your partner around her shoulders and chest *(far right)*. Reverse direction and roll on your back.

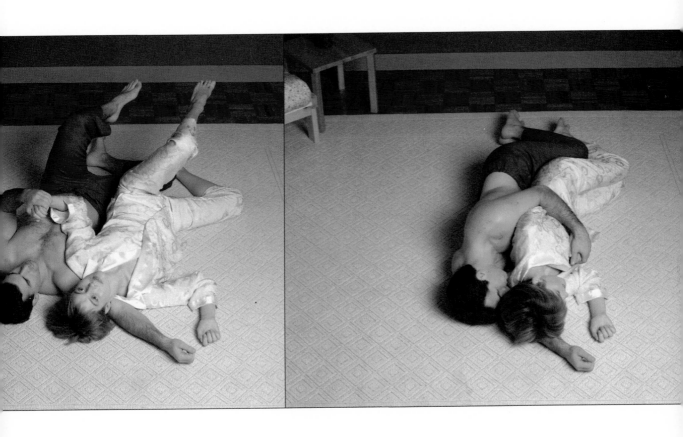

Movement/4

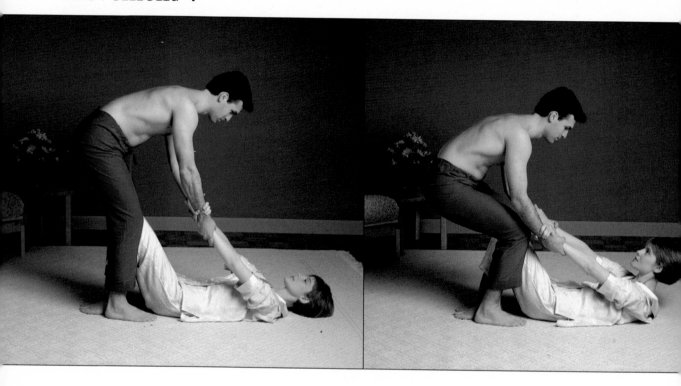

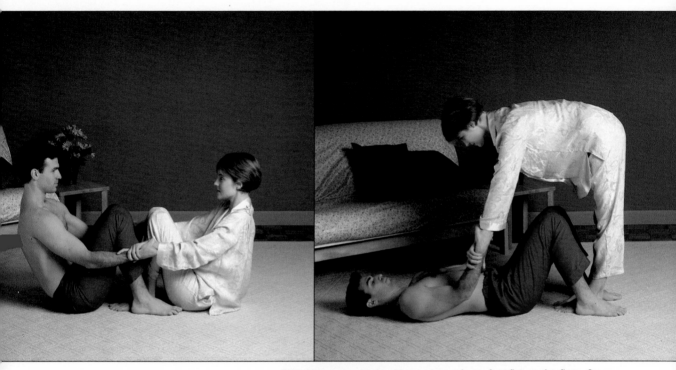

SHE: Lie on your back with your knees bent, feet flat on the floor. Grasp his forearms. **HE**: Stand at your partner's feet. Lean over her with your knees flexed and grasp her forearms *(left)*. **SHE**: Lift your head and upper back off the floor. **HE**: Crouch and pull back on your partner's arms *(second from left)*. **SHE**: Rise to a sitting position. **HE**: Lower yourself to a sitting position *(third from left)*. **SHE**: Stand bending over him without letting go of his arms. **HE**: Lean back so that your head and shoulders rest on the floor *(above)*.

Movement/5

SHE: Kneel, fold your arms under you and touch your forehead to the floor. **HE**: Kneel behind her and lean over her, bringing your arms around her so that your hands clasp her wrists. Let your face rest on her upper back *(top left)*. **SHE**: Lift your torso, keeping your hands at waist level. **HE**: Let her movement push you up. Be sure to keep your face against her back *(top right)*. **SHE**: Extend your arms to the side as you continue lifting your torso. **HE**: Lift your head and continue to rise as she rises, letting your arms extend to the sides *(bottom left)*. **SHE**: Bring yourself to an upright position, your arms raised to form a wide V. **HE**: Sit up on your knees, keeping your hands around her wrists or touching the sides of her hands *(bottom right)*.

CHAPTER FOUR

Trace Minerals

Zinc, iodine and other microminerals essential for your senses

T here are no foods that act as aphrodisiacs to improve your sex life. But some reputed aphrodisiacs do contain minerals that are related to the proper functioning of your sexual organs and the health of your senses. Oysters, for instance, contain zinc, which you need to maintain your senses of smell and taste as well as for the development of your reproductive capacity. Zinc is one of 22 essential minerals that your diet must provide for the proper functioning of your body.

Scientists classify essential minerals according to the amount people need: Macrominerals — including calcium, phosphorus, sodium, chlorine, magnesium, potassium and sulfur — are required in amounts ranging from a few tenths of a gram to one or more grams per day. Essential microminerals, or trace elements, are required in amounts ranging from millionths to thousandths of a gram.

Enough is known about the microminerals zinc, iron and iodine for the Food and Nutrition Board of the National Academy of Sciences to develop Recommended Dietary Allowances (RDAs) for them. The roles played by six others — chromium, copper, fluorine, manganese, molybdenum and selenium — are not as well understood; therefore, they have been assigned "safe and adequate" daily ranges instead of specific RDAs. The best sources of trace minerals are foods, except for fluorine, which fluoridated water provides. Not only are supplements unnecessary, but excessive amounts can be toxic — and may even be fatal, in the case of selenium.

Zinc supplements have been mistakenly promoted as an aid for treating infertility and impotence. These erroneous claims may have originated from a misinterpretation of studies of Middle Eastern adolescent boys whose diets lacked adequate zinc and who suffered from stunted growth and sexual immaturity. The boys were cured with zinc supplements and diet therapy. In addition to maintaining the senses of smell and taste, zinc is essential for healthy bones, hair and skin, and for forming more than 70 enzymes — chemicals with a multitude of roles. You will receive your recommended allowance of zinc by consuming seafood, whole grains, milk, red meat and eggs.

The trace element manganese is necessary for reproduction, energy metabolism, the development of the musculoskeletal system and the functioning of the nervous system. Manganese-rich foods include nuts, whole-grain breads and cereals, vegetables and fruit. Copper and iron are both required for the synthesis of hemoglobin, the molecule in red blood cells that carries oxygen. As a component of vitamin B_{12}, the trace element cobalt also plays an essential role in the formation of red blood cells, but because it is a part of vitamin B_{12}, no "safe and adequate" level has been established for it. Adequate copper may help protect against heart disease, while a lack of copper may elevate blood cholesterol. Nutritionists estimate that 75 percent of Americans receive less copper than they need because they seldom consume organ meats and shellfish, among the best sources of copper, along with legumes and whole grains. Despite being widely available in foods, iron is often not well absorbed. (Adequate vitamin C can more than double the absorption of iron, but excessive amounts of vitamin C interfere with copper absorption.) Some of the best food sources of iron are liver and other red meat, fish, poultry, legumes, whole grains, prunes and raisins.

Selenium, which used to be considered poisonous in any amount, actually protects your body against toxic intakes of the poisonous metals cadmium and mercury. It is necessary for the functioning of the heart muscle and is an antioxidant that protects tissue.

Like most other trace minerals, chromium is involved in enzyme functions, specifically aiding in the conversion of fat, protein and carbohydrates into energy. Recent studies suggest that chromium may help prevent cardiovascular disease by regulating blood lipid levels. Among the best sources are whole grains and cereals, vegetables, fruits, meat and eggs.

The role of fluorine in preventing tooth decay has long been recog-

The Basic Guidelines

For a moderately active adult, the National Institutes of Health recommends a diet that is low in fat, high in carbohydrates and moderate in protein. The institutes' guidelines suggest that no more than 30 percent of your calories come from fat, that 55 to 60 percent come from carbohydrates and that no more than 15 percent come from protein. A gram of fat equals nine calories, while a gram of protein or carbohydrate equals four calories; therefore, if you eat 2,100 calories a day, you should consume approximately 60 grams of fat, 315 grams of carbohydrate and no more than 75 grams of protein daily. If you follow a lowfat/high-carbohydrate diet, your chance of developing heart disease, cancer and other life-threatening diseases may be considerably reduced.

◆ The nutrition charts that accompany each of the lowfat/high-carbohydrate recipes in this book include the number of calories per serving, the number of grams of fat, carbohydrate and protein in a serving, and the percentage of calories derived from each of these nutrients. In addition, the charts provide the amount of calcium, iron and sodium per serving.

◆ Calcium deficiency may be associated with periodontal disease — which attacks the mouth's bones and tissues, including the gums — in both men and women, and with osteoporosis, or bone shrinking and weakening, in the elderly. The deficiency may also contribute to high blood pressure. The recommended daily allowance for calcium is 800 milligrams a day for men and women. Pregnant and lactating women are advised to consume 1,200 milligrams daily; a National Institutes of Health consensus panel recommends that postmenopausal women consume 1,200 to 1,500 milligrams of calcium daily.

◆ Although one way you can reduce your fat intake is to cut your consumption of red meat, you should make sure that you get your necessary iron from other sources. The Food and Nutrition Board of the National Academy of Sciences suggests a minimum of 10 milligrams of iron per day for men and 18 milligrams for women between the ages of 11 and 50.

◆ High sodium intake is associated with high blood pressure. Most adults should restrict sodium intake to between 2,000 and 2,500 milligrams a day, according to the National Academy of Sciences. One way to keep sodium consumption in check is not to add table salt to food.

nized; research suggests that fluorine is also essential for growth and reproduction, and for the prevention of osteoporosis by restricting bone demineralization. In addition to fluoridated water, food sources include fish and some vegetables.

Molybdenum takes part in the enzyme reactions in amino-acid metabolism and in mobilizing iron from storage in the liver. Recent studies suggest that molybdenum may also promote the retention of fluorine. Legumes, whole grains and meat contain molybdenum.

Iodine is contained in the hormones that regulate many aspects of growth and development. It plays a role in reproduction and cellular metabolism. Seafood is a good source of iodine.

The recipes on the following 14 pages provide dishes that are high in one or more essential minerals. Because they work interdependently, the safest way to maintain an effective balance among them is by consuming a varied diet.

Sweet Potato Pancakes

Breakfast

SWEET POTATO PANCAKES

The eggs, potatoes, vegetable oil and brown sugar in this recipe are all good sources of chromium.

CALORIES per serving	158
60% Carbohydrate	24 g
8% Protein	3 g
32% Fat	6 g
CALCIUM	37 mg
IRON	1 mg
SODIUM	26 mg

1/3 cup unbleached
  all-purpose flour
1/4 cup skim milk
1 egg, beaten
2 tablespoons brown sugar

1/2 teaspoon ground ginger
1 pound sweet potatoes,
  peeled and grated (4 cups)
1/4 cup chopped scallions
2 tablespoons vegetable oil

In a large bowl beat together the flour, milk, egg, sugar and ginger. Stir in the potatoes and scallions. In a large nonstick skillet, heat 1 1/2 teaspoons of oil over medium-high heat until it barely begins to smoke. Drop six 1/4-cup portions of the potato mixture into the skillet and cook for 1 minute. Using a spatula, flatten the mixture into 1/4-inch-thick cakes, then reduce the heat to medium and cook for 2 to 3 minutes more. Turn the pancakes, add 1 1/2 teaspoons of oil and cook for another 5 minutes, shaking the pan to keep the pancakes from sticking.

Turn the pancakes again and drizzle 2 to 3 tablespoons of water into the pan. Increase the heat to medium-high and cook, pressing the pancakes with the spatula to brown them evenly, for 2 minutes more, or until the pancakes are golden brown all over. Transfer the pancakes to a platter and cover loosely with foil. Repeat with the remaining potato mixture, divide the pancakes among 6 plates and serve. Makes 6 servings

PEAR MILK SHAKE

Dairy products, such as yogurt and skim milk, may contain significant amounts of iodine and are excellent sources of calcium.

1 ripe Bartlett pear	1/4 cup Yogurt Cheese
2 teaspoons maple syrup	(see page 140)
1/4 teaspoon almond extract	1/4 cup skim milk

Peel, core and coarsely dice the pear; you should have about 1 cup. Pour just enough water into the bottom pan of a double boiler so that the water will not touch the top pan and bring it to a simmer. Place the pear, maple syrup and almond extract in the top pan, cover and cook for 10 minutes, or until the pear is very tender. Remove the pan from the heat and let the pear mixture cool slightly, then cover the pan and refrigerate until well chilled.

Place the Yogurt Cheese in a blender and process for 5 seconds to soften it. Add the pear mixture and process for 5 seconds, or until smooth. Add the milk, process for 5 seconds more and serve. Makes 1 serving

CALORIES per serving	216
75% Carbohydrate	42 g
15% Protein	8 g
10% Fat	3 g
CALCIUM	264 mg
IRON	1 mg
SODIUM	89 mg

CORNMEAL MUFFINS

Liver is one of the best sources of zinc, but milk, eggs and vegetable oils — such as those in margarine — can supply this mineral for those who eat no meat. Cornmeal is a good source of chromium.

1/2 cup buttermilk	1/3 cup unbleached
1 tablespoon plus 1 teaspoon	all-purpose flour
unsalted butter or margarine,	1/2 cup yellow cornmeal
melted and cooled	1/4 cup packed brown sugar
1 egg, beaten	2 teaspoons baking powder
	Pinch of salt

Preheat the oven to 375° F. Line 12 muffin tin cups with paper liners. In a medium-size bowl stir together the buttermilk, butter and egg until blended. In another medium-size bowl combine the flour, cornmeal, sugar, baking powder and salt. Add the dry ingredients to the buttermilk mixture and stir just to combine; do not overmix. Divide the batter among the muffin tin cups and bake for 20 minutes, or until the muffins are golden brown and a toothpick inserted into the center of a muffin comes out clean. Makes 12 muffins

CALORIES per muffin	73
67% Carbohydrate	12 g
9% Protein	2 g
24% Fat	2 g
CALCIUM	55 mg
IRON	.5 mg
SODIUM	100 mg

129

BANANA OAT SHAKE

This thick milk shake gets its rich texture from cooked oatmeal rather than from high-fat ingredients. Oats and wheat germ are good sources of molybdenum, an element essential to food metabolism.

CALORIES per serving	143
79% Carbohydrate	29 g
14% Protein	5 g
7% Fat	1 g
CALCIUM	114 mg
IRON	1 mg
SODIUM	45 mg

1/2 cup cooked oatmeal, well chilled
1 frozen banana, peeled and cut into chunks
2/3 cup skim milk

2 teaspoons brown sugar
1 teaspoon wheat germ
1/2 teaspoon vanilla extract
2 to 3 ice cubes (optional)

Place the oatmeal in a blender and process for 20 seconds, or until smooth. Add the banana and process for another 10 to 15 seconds, or until smooth. Add the milk, sugar, wheat germ and vanilla, and the ice cubes if using them, and process for 10 seconds more, or until the mixture is thick and smoothly blended. Divide the shake between 2 glasses and serve. Makes 2 servings

STEAMED BROWN BREAD WITH APRICOTS

Apricots, molasses and whole-wheat flour are good sources of naturally occurring iron. Most white flour and cornmeal is iron-enriched.

Vegetable cooking spray
1 cup rye flour
1/2 cup whole-wheat flour
1/2 cup unbleached all-purpose flour
1 cup yellow cornmeal
2 1/2 teaspoons baking soda

Pinch of salt
2 cups buttermilk
2/3 cup molasses
2/3 cup coarsely chopped dried apricots
1 tablespoon brown sugar
1 tablespoon margarine, melted

CALORIES per 2-slice serving	196
83% Carbohydrate	41 g
9% Protein	5 g
8% Fat	2 g
CALCIUM	88 mg
IRON	2 mg
SODIUM	241 mg

Lightly spray four clean 14-ounce cans and their detached lids with cooking spray; set aside. In a large bowl stir together the rye, whole-wheat and all-purpose flours, the cornmeal, baking soda and salt, and make a well in the center. In a medium-size bowl stir together the buttermilk, molasses, apricots, sugar and margarine, and add this mixture to the dry ingredients. Stir just until the dry ingredients are incorporated; do not overmix. Divide the batter among the cans, filling them about two thirds full. Tap the cans on the counter to settle the batter. Cover each can with its lid (which may fall in and rest on the batter) and secure the lid with string, encircling the can twice from top to bottom. Or, cover the top of each can with a large double sheet of foil. Press it firmly around the can and tie it tightly around the rim.

Stand the cans on a trivet in a deep pot or Dutch oven and add boiling water to a depth of 1 inch. Cover the pot and steam the breads over low heat for 3 hours, checking occasionally to be sure that the water continues to simmer and adding more boiling water if the level drops below 1 inch.

Place the cans upside down on a rack to cool for 10 minutes, then remove the lids. If the loaves do not slip out easily, remove the bottoms of the cans. To serve, cut each loaf into six slices and serve warm, at room temperature or toasted. Uncut loaves can be tightly wrapped in plastic bags and eaten within 2 days of baking, or they can be frozen. Makes 12 servings

Lunch

ASPARAGUS AND PEPPERS WITH CRAB

Minerals are water-soluble and may be lost in the cooking liquid, so use as little liquid as possible and include it in the finished dish.

1 cup brown rice
3/4 cup low-sodium chicken stock
2 tablespoons Oriental sesame oil
2 teaspoons cornstarch
1 teaspoon dry sherry
3/4 teaspoon sugar

2 pounds asparagus, trimmed
2 cups thinly sliced red bell
  peppers
1/3 cup lump crabmeat
1 egg white, beaten
2/3 cup chopped scallions

CALORIES per serving	300
59% Carbohydrate	46 g
16% Protein	12 g
25% Fat	9 g
CALCIUM	72 mg
IRON	3 mg
SODIUM	67 mg

Bring 2 cups of water to a boil in a medium-size saucepan. Stir in the rice, cover the pan, reduce the heat to low and cook for 40 minutes, or until the rice is tender and all the water is absorbed; remove from the heat and set aside.

In a large skillet combine the stock, oil, cornstarch, sherry, sugar and 2 tablespoons of water and stir until blended. Bring the mixture to a boil over medium-high heat, then add the asparagus and peppers. Reduce the heat to low, cover the skillet and simmer for 2 minutes, or until the asparagus is crisp-tender. Divide the rice among 4 plates. Using a slotted spatula, quickly drain the vegetables and arrange them on the rice. Scatter one fourth of the crabmeat over each serving. For the sauce, return the cooking liquid to a boil, stir in the egg white and scallions, and cook, stirring, for just 2 to 3 seconds, or until the egg white turns opaque. Immediately pour the sauce over the vegetables and crabmeat, and serve. Makes 4 servings

Asparagus and Peppers with Crab

CURRIED SHRIMP FOLD-UPS

Although iodized salt is the primary iodine source in the American diet, shellfish are among the best sources of this trace mineral.

CALORIES per serving	202
51% Carbohydrate	27 g
22% Protein	11 g
27% Fat	6 g
CALCIUM	77 mg
IRON	3 mg
SODIUM	373 mg

2 teaspoons curry powder
1 teaspoon cornstarch
1 teaspoon tamari
1 tablespoon vegetable oil
1/4 cup chopped shallots
1 tablespoon minced
  fresh ginger
1 garlic clove, minced

1/4 pound peeled, deveined
  shrimp, coarsely chopped
1/2 cup chopped celery
1/2 cup chopped green bell
  pepper
8 slices soft, fresh
  whole-wheat bread
1 teaspoon margarine

In a small bowl combine the curry powder, cornstarch, tamari and 3 tablespoons of water and stir until smooth; set aside. Heat the oil in a medium-size nonstick skillet over medium heat. Add the shallots, ginger and garlic and sauté for 1 minute, or until the garlic just begins to brown. Add the shrimp, celery and bell pepper, and cook, stirring frequently, for 1 to 2 minutes, or just until the shrimp turn orange. Increase the heat to high. Stir the cornstarch mixture, then add it to the skillet and cook for 10 seconds, or until the liquid thickens. (Add up to 1 tablespoon of water if it seems too thick.) Remove the skillet from the heat.

Preheat the oven to 400° F. Place 2 rounded tablespoonsful of the shrimp mixture on one half of each slice of bread, then fold the bread over to make a sandwich and secure with a toothpick. Place the sandwiches on a baking sheet and cover them with a damp kitchen towel. Melt the margarine in a small saucepan over medium-low heat. Brush the sandwiches with margarine, then heat them in the oven for 5 minutes, or until lightly browned. Divide the sandwiches among 4 plates and serve.   Makes 4 servings

Note: Tamari, a thick, mellow, unrefined soy sauce, is sold in health-food shops and Oriental grocery stores.

SCALLION-CHEESE BREAD

This bread adds almost all the trace minerals to your meal. Cheddar cheese alone provides chromium, copper, selenium and zinc.

CALORIES per slice	106
69% Carbohydrate	19 g
14% Protein	4 g
17% Fat	2 g
CALCIUM	39 mg
IRON	1 mg
SODIUM	103 mg

1/2 cup buttermilk
2 tablespoons lemon juice
1 tablespoon margarine
1 package dry yeast
  (2 teaspoons)
1 1/2 cups whole-wheat flour,
  approximately

1 1/2 cups unbleached
  all-purpose flour
1 tablespoon sugar
1/2 teaspoon salt
1 cup chopped scallions
1 1/2 ounces sharp Cheddar
  cheese, grated (scant 1/2 cup)

Combine the buttermilk, lemon juice and margarine in a small skillet over medium heat, and warm the mixture just until tepid; remove from the heat and set aside. Place the yeast in a small bowl and add 1/3 cup of warm water

(105-115° F); set aside for 5 minutes. Meanwhile, in a large bowl combine 1 1/2 cups of whole-wheat flour, the all-purpose flour, sugar and salt, and make a well in the center.

Pour the buttermilk and yeast mixtures into the dry ingredients and stir to form a dough. Turn the dough out on a lightly floured surface and knead it for 8 to 10 minutes, or until smooth and elastic. Return the dough to the bowl, cover with a damp kitchen towel and set aside in a draft-free place to rise for 1 hour, or until doubled in bulk.

Punch down the dough and knead it for 2 minutes. Return the dough to the bowl, cover and let it rise for 45 minutes, or until almost doubled in bulk.

Punch down the dough again and roll it out on a lightly floured surface to a 10 x 15-inch rectangle. Sprinkle the scallions and cheese evenly over the dough. Starting with a long edge, roll up the dough and filling, jelly-roll fashion, as tightly as possible. Tuck in the ends to seal them and place the bread seam-side down on a baking sheet to rise, uncovered, for 30 minutes.

Preheat the oven to 350° F. Bake the bread for 30 to 40 minutes, or until it is golden brown and sounds hollow when tapped. Cool the bread on a rack for at least 10 minutes, then cut it into 16 slices and serve.   Makes 16 servings

CITRUS-PICKLED VEGETABLE SALAD

Iron is best absorbed by the body in the presence of acid, which the citrus juices in this recipe supply. Eating an acidic dish like this also enhances the body's utilization of iron from other foods eaten at the same meal.

1/4 cup orange juice	2 cups yellow squash, sliced
1 teaspoon grated orange peel	1/4 inch thick
2 tablespoons lime juice	1 tablespoon plus 2 teaspoons
1 teaspoon grated lime peel	walnut oil
1 tablespoon brown sugar	1/4 teaspoon minced garlic
1/2 teaspoon ground cinnamon	1 cup chopped scallions
2 cups cauliflower florets	1/2 cup cooked kidney beans
2 cups green beans, cut into	(1/4 cup dried)
2-inch lengths	Four 1-ounce whole-wheat rolls

Bring 2 cups of water to a boil in a medium-size saucepan. Meanwhile, for the marinade, in a small bowl stir together the orange juice and peel, lime juice and peel, sugar and cinnamon; set aside. Add the cauliflower, green beans and squash to the boiling water. When the water returns to a boil, cover the pan, reduce the heat to low and simmer for 1 to 2 minutes, or until the vegetables are crisp-tender. Drain the vegetables in a colander and cool under cold running water; set aside.

Heat the oil in a small skillet over medium heat, add the garlic and cook for 5 minutes, or until the garlic begins to brown; remove the skillet from the heat and set aside. Place the vegetables in a large bowl, add the marinade, the oil and garlic, scallions and kidney beans, and stir well. Cover the bowl and set the salad aside at room temperature to marinate for at least 2 hours, stirring occasionally. For a more intense flavor, marinate the vegetables overnight in the refrigerator. Serve the salad chilled or at room temperature, and warm the rolls if desired.   Makes 4 servings

CALORIES per serving	230
60% Carbohydrate	37 g
14% Protein	9 g
26% Fat	7 g
CALCIUM	115 mg
IRON	4 mg
SODIUM	166 mg

Turkey-Chestnut Salad

Dinner

. . . .

TURKEY-CHESTNUT SALAD

Turkey is a good source of zinc. A serving of this filling main-dish salad provides one gram of this mineral.

CALORIES per serving	482
62% Carbohydrate	75 g
16% Protein	20 g
22% Fat	12 g
CALCIUM	145 mg
IRON	6 mg
SODIUM	362 mg

10 ounces fresh chestnuts in
  shell (about 36 chestnuts)
4 slices whole-wheat bread
2 tablespoons plus
  2 teaspoons margarine
1/4 cup unbleached
  all-purpose flour
2 cups low-sodium chicken stock
2 cups diced yellow bell peppers

1 1/3 cups diced celery
3/4 teaspoon dried thyme
1/4 teaspoon ground pepper
8 cups Romaine, loosely packed,
  torn into bite-size pieces
2 cups sliced, cooked beets
1/4 pound skinless cooked
  turkey breast, thinly sliced

Using a sharp paring knife, cut an X on one flat side of each chestnut. Bring 3 cups of water to a boil in a medium-size saucepan over medium-high heat and add the chestnuts. When the water returns to a boil, reduce the heat to medium-low, partially cover the pan and cook for 20 minutes, or until the chestnuts are tender when pierced with a knife. Meanwhile, preheat the oven to 375° F. Cut the bread into 1/4-inch cubes, spread the cubes on a baking sheet and bake for 5 minutes, or until crisp and golden; set aside to cool.

When the chestnuts are cooked, transfer them to a colander and cool under cold running water. Remove and discard the outer shell and inner skin. Break the chestnuts in half if they do not break into pieces as they are peeled; cover the chestnuts loosely with foil and set aside.

For the dressing, melt the margarine in a medium-size saucepan over medium heat, add the flour, and cook, stirring, until the mixture forms a smooth paste. Gradually stir in the stock, bring to a boil and cook, stirring constantly, for 1 minute, or until the mixture is thickened. Stir in the bell peppers, celery, thyme and ground pepper, and reduce the heat to medium-low. Partially cover the pan and simmer the mixture for 1 to 2 minutes, or until the vegetables are just crisp-tender.

To serve, divide the Romaine among 4 plates. Arrange the beets and turkey on the Romaine, scatter the chestnuts and croutons on top and spoon the dressing over the salads.　　　　　　　　　　　　　Makes 4 servings

MUSTARD CHICKEN AND VEGETABLES ON PITA

Manganese, which is essential for proper functioning of the nervous system and for bone development, is found in most vegetables.

1/4 pound skinless, boneless chicken breast	1/2 pound asparagus
1 tablespoon plus 1 teaspoon coarse Dijon mustard	1/2 cup low-sodium chicken stock
1/2 pound red onions	1 tablespoon sherry
1 ounce shallots	1 tablespoon cornstarch
1/2 pound carrots	Eight 1-ounce pita breads
	3 tablespoons margarine
	1/4 teaspoon ground pepper

Remove and discard any visible fat from the chicken. Slice the chicken 1/4 inch thick and toss the slices with 1 tablespoon of mustard in a medium-size bowl. Cover loosely with plastic wrap and set aside. Peel, trim and slice the onions and shallots. Wash and trim the carrots and asparagus; cut the carrots diagonally into 1/4-inch-thick slices and cut the asparagus into 1 1/2-inch lengths; set aside. In a small bowl combine the stock, sherry, cornstarch and remaining mustard; set aside.

Preheat the oven to 400° F. Place the pita breads on a baking sheet and set aside. Melt 1 tablespoon of margarine in a large nonstick skillet over medium-high heat, add the chicken and sauté for 2 to 3 minutes, or just until the chicken turns white. Transfer the chicken to a clean bowl, cover and set aside. Wipe out the skillet with paper towels.

Heat the pita breads in the oven for 5 minutes, or just until crisp, then wrap them loosely in foil to keep warm. Meanwhile, melt the remaining margarine over medium-high heat and add the onion and shallots. Reduce the heat to medium and sauté for 5 minutes, or until the onions are translucent and beginning to brown. Add the carrots and asparagus, and sauté for 2 to 3 minutes more. Increase the heat to high. Stir the cornstarch mixture and add it to the skillet, stirring constantly. Add the chicken and pepper, and cook, stirring, for about 2 minutes, or until the chicken is heated through and the sauce has thickened. Place each pita bread on a plate, top with the chicken mixture and serve.　　　　　　　　　　　　　Makes 8 servings

CALORIES per serving	176
58% Carbohydrate	25 g
16% Protein	7 g
26% Fat	5 g
CALCIUM	26 mg
IRON	1 mg
SODIUM	329 mg

CALORIES per serving	174
87% Carbohydrate	42 g
6% Protein	3 g
7% Fat	2 g
CALCIUM	70 mg
IRON	2 mg
SODIUM	191 mg

PINEAPPLE GAZPACHO

The six kinds of fruits and vegetables in this Spanish-inspired soup all supply chromium, which aids the hormone insulin in distributing glucose to the body's cells.

2 medium-size cucumbers
6 cups fresh pineapple, or drained
   juice-packed pineapple chunks
One 14-ounce can plum tomatoes

1 red bell pepper
1/2 cup orange juice
3 tablespoons lemon juice
1/4 cup chopped fresh mint

Wash, halve and seed the cucumbers, and cut them into chunks. Process the cucumbers and pineapple in a food processor or blender for 45 seconds, or until finely chopped, pulsing the machine on and off. Add the tomatoes and their liquid, and process for 15 seconds; transfer to a serving bowl.

   Stem and seed the pepper, cut it into large chunks and process it with the orange juice, lemon juice and mint for 5 seconds. Add this mixture to the serving bowl and stir to combine. Cover the bowl and refrigerate the gazpacho for 4 hours, or until the soup is well chilled. Just before serving, stir the gazpacho to reblend it, then divide it among 4 bowls.   Makes 4 servings

PASTA AND VEGETABLES WITH GOAT-CHEESE SAUCE

Enriched pasta contains significantly more iron than nonenriched pasta.

1/2 pound asparagus
1 medium-size cucumber
1 yellow bell pepper
3/4 cup low-sodium chicken stock
2 teaspoons cornstarch
2 tablespoons margarine
1 cup thinly sliced shallots

1/4 cup lowfat cottage
   cheese (1%)
2 ounces mild goat cheese
1/2 pound enriched pasta shells
2 tablespoons chopped fresh basil
White pepper

Wash and trim the asparagus and cucumber. Cut the asparagus into 2-inch lengths; halve the unpeeled cucumber lengthwise, then cut it into 1/4-inch-thick slices. Wash, stem and seed the bell pepper, and cut it into 3/4-inch squares. Stir together the stock and cornstarch in a small bowl; set aside.

   Melt the margarine in a medium-size skillet over medium heat, add the shallots and sauté for 2 minutes, or until translucent. Add the vegetables and cook, stirring, for 1 minute, then increase the heat to high. Stir the cornstarch mixture and add it to the skillet. Bring the mixture to a boil, stirring constantly, and cook for 2 minutes, or until the asparagus is crisp-tender. Remove the skillet from the heat and carefully pour off the cooking liquid into a small bowl; cover with foil to keep warm. Partially cover the skillet and set aside.

   Bring a large pot of water to a boil. Meanwhile, place the cheeses in a blender. With the machine running, drizzle in the cooking liquid and process for 5 to 10 seconds, or until the mixure forms a smooth sauce; set aside. Cook the pasta in the boiling water for 10 to 12 minutes, or according to the package directions, until al dente. Drain the pasta thoroughly, transfer it to a large serving bowl and add the vegetables, sauce and basil. Toss the mixture, add pepper to taste and serve.   Makes 4 servings

CALORIES per serving	368
60% Carbohydrate	55 g
15% Protein	14 g
25% Fat	10 g
CALCIUM	65 mg
IRON	3 mg
SODIUM	282 mg

Desserts

· · · · · · · · · · · · · · · ·

APPLE-RAISIN PIE

Butter, oats and cinnamon are all good sources of selenium.

1 cup unbleached all-purpose flour, approximately	1 1/3 cups golden raisins
5 tablespoons sugar	1/3 cup dry bread crumbs
1/4 cup rolled oats	1 tablespoon grated lemon peel
Pinch of salt	1 tablespoon lemon juice
5 tablespoons butter	1/2 teaspoon ground allspice
2 large apples	1/4 teaspoon ground cinnamon

Combine 1 cup of flour, 4 tablespoons of sugar, the oats and salt in a food processor. Add the butter while pulsing the machine on and off for 10 seconds, or until the mixture resembles cornmeal. With the machine running, drizzle in 2 to 3 tablespoons of cold water and process for 5 seconds, or until the mixture begins to clump together. With your hands, form the dough into a ball; set aside. (To mix by hand, see Buckwheat Crackers, page 141.)

Grate the unpeeled apples into a large bowl. Add the raisins, bread crumbs, lemon peel and juice, allspice, cinnamon and remaining sugar, and mix well.

Preheat the oven to 450° F. Dust the work surface and a rolling pin with flour. Cut off two thirds of the dough, roll it out into a 10-inch circle and press it into an 8-inch pie plate or quiche pan; flute the edges. Roll out the remaining dough into a 6 x 6-inch square and cut it into 8 equal strips. Spoon the filling into the pastry shell and use the pastry strips to form a lattice on top. Bake the pie for 10 minutes, then reduce the oven temperature to 350° F. and bake for 15 minutes more, or until the crust is golden. Let the pie cool on a rack for at least 5 minutes, then cut it into 8 wedges and serve.   Makes 8 servings

CALORIES per serving	293
71% Carbohydrate	55 g
5% Protein	4 g
24% Fat	8 g
CALCIUM	32 mg
IRON	1 mg
SODIUM	134 mg

Apple-Raisin Pie

QUINOA PUDDING

Quinoa, a South American grain that resembles millet, has been described by the National Academy of Sciences as "one of the best sources of protein in the vegetable kingdom." It is also a good source of iron, zinc and B vitamins. You can find quinoa at health-food stores.

1/2 cup quinoa	1 teaspoon almond extract
2 eggs	1 cup cooked brown rice
1 cup skim milk	1/2 cup chopped dried figs
3 tablespoons brown sugar	1/4 cup rolled oats

Place the quinoa in a bowl and rinse it thoroughly in several changes of cold water. (Quinoa may have a slight residue of its natural bitter-tasting coating; rinsing will remove it.) Skim off and discard any grains or fragments that float to the surface. Place the quinoa in a medium-size saucepan with 1 cup of water and bring to a boil over medium-high heat. Cover the pan, reduce the heat to low and simmer for 10 to 15 minutes, or until the quinoa is transparent and all the water is absorbed. Remove the pan from the heat and set aside.

Preheat the oven to 375° F. Beat the eggs in a medium-size bowl. Stir in the milk, sugar and almond extract, then add the quinoa, rice, figs and oats, and stir well. Pour the mixture into a deep 1 1/2-quart baking dish and place it in a larger pan. Add enough boiling water to the pan to reach halfway up the side of the baking dish. Bake the pudding for 45 minutes, or until set and golden on top. Let the pudding cool for 10 minutes and serve.   Makes 6 servings

CALORIES per serving	217
72% Carbohydrate	40 g
14% Protein	8 g
14% Fat	3 g
CALCIUM	111 mg
IRON	3 mg
SODIUM	50 mg

PINEAPPLE-BANANA CAKE

Cobalt is a component of vitamin B_{12}. This vitamin, found in eggs and milk, is an essential factor in the formation of red blood cells.

Vegetable cooking spray	2 eggs
1 1/2 cups unbleached	1 ripe banana, peeled and
all-purpose flour, approximately	mashed
1/2 teaspoon baking powder	1/2 cup drained juice-packed
1/4 teaspoon baking soda	pineapple chunks
1/4 teaspoon salt	1/2 teaspoon vanilla extract
1/4 cup margarine, softened	1/4 cup buttermilk
1/2 cup packed brown sugar	

Preheat the oven to 375° F. Lightly spray an 8-inch round cake pan with cooking spray and dust it lightly with flour; set aside. In a medium-size bowl combine 1 1/2 cups of flour, the baking powder, baking soda and salt. In a large bowl, using an electric mixer, cream the margarine, then add the sugar and continue beating for 1 minute, or until well blended. Add the eggs one at a time, beating well after each addition. Add the banana, pineapple, vanilla and half of the flour mixture, and beat at low speed for 15 seconds. Beat in the buttermilk, then add the remaining flour mixture and beat just until incorporated. Pour the batter into the pan and bake for 30 minutes, or until the cake is golden on top and pulls away from the sides of the pan; a toothpick inserted into the cake should come out clean. Let the cake cool in the pan on a rack for 5 minutes, then turn it out to cool completely.   Makes 8 servings

CALORIES per serving	235
64% Carbohydrate	38 g
7% Protein	5 g
29% Fat	8 g
CALCIUM	50 mg
IRON	2 mg
SODIUM	216 mg

FRUIT PUDDING

Manganese, found in strawberries and raspberries, activates enzymes in the synthesis of protein.

3/4 cup hulled, sliced strawberries	5 tablespoons unbleached all-purpose flour
1/2 cup raspberries	1 teaspoon grated lime peel
1 cup peeled, sliced peaches (see Note)	2 tablespoons whipped margarine, cut into small pieces
2 tablespoons sugar	1/4 teaspoon ground cinnamon
1 teaspoon cornstarch	

Preheat the oven to 350° F. Combine the strawberries, raspberries, peaches, 1 tablespoon of sugar, the cornstarch and 3 tablespoons of water in a medium-size saucepan, and cook over medium heat for 5 minutes; transfer the mixture to an 8-inch square baking pan and set aside. Combine the flour, lime peel and remaining sugar in a small bowl, then blend in the margarine with a pastry blender or 2 knives to form a crumbly mixture. Sprinkle the topping evenly over the fruit and bake for 25 minutes, or until bubbly. Let the pudding cool for 5 minutes, then sprinkle with cinnamon and serve.   Makes 2 servings

Note: Unsweetened frozen berries and peaches can be substituted when the fresh fruits are out of season.

CALORIES per serving	274
67% Carbohydrate	46 g
5% Protein	3 g
28% Fat	9 g
CALCIUM	27 mg
IRON	1 mg
SODIUM	71 mg

MOCHA LOAF CAKE

Instant coffee might seem an unlikely nutrient source, but it supplies a considerable amount of chromium, a trace mineral that helps produce energy from the foods you eat.

Vegetable cooking spray	2 teaspoons baking powder
1 2/3 cups unbleached all-purpose flour, approximately	Pinch of salt
1/4 cup skim milk	1/2 pound ripe pears, peeled, cored and grated
1 ounce unsweetened chocolate	1/2 cup packed brown sugar
2 teaspoons instant coffee granules or powder	1/2 cup lowfat cottage cheese (1%)
1 teaspoon vanilla extract	2 eggs, beaten

Preheat the oven to 375° F. Spray a 9 x 5-inch loaf pan with cooking spray and dust it lightly with flour; set aside.

   Heat the milk, chocolate, coffee and vanilla in a small saucepan over low heat, stirring occasionally, for 5 minutes, or until the chocolate melts. Meanwhile, in a medium-size bowl combine 1 2/3 cups of flour, the baking powder and salt; set aside. In a small bowl stir together the pears, sugar, cottage cheese and eggs. Stir in the milk mixture. Make a well in the dry ingredients, pour in the pear mixture and fold together with a rubber spatula just until the dry ingredients are incorporated; do not overmix. Pour the batter into the pan and bake for 50 minutes, or until a toothpick inserted into the cake comes out clean. Let the cake cool in the pan on a rack for 5 minutes, then turn it out to cool completely.   Makes 8 servings

CALORIES per slice	216
72% Carbohydrate	39 g
12% Protein	7 g
16% Fat	4 g
CALCIUM	100 mg
IRON	3 mg
SODIUM	207 mg

Snacks
·············

YOGURT CHEESE WITH PEPPER AND HERBS

The black pepper that flavors this lowfat spread is a rich source of copper, which facilitates the body's absorption of iron.

2 cups plain lowfat yogurt
3/4 teaspoon coarsely ground
   black pepper
1/4 teaspoon salt

3 tablespoons chopped
   fresh chives
48 Buckwheat Crackers
   (recipe follows)

CALORIES per serving	219
57% Carbohydrate	31 g
17% Protein	9 g
26% Fat	6 g
CALCIUM	201 mg
IRON	1 mg
SODIUM	347 mg

Place a cheesecloth-lined strainer over a bowl. Spoon the yogurt into the strainer, cover with plastic wrap and refrigerate for 24 hours, or until the yogurt is the consistency of thick sour cream. (Discard the whey, or reserve it to use in soups or in baking recipes requiring buttermilk or sour milk.) Transfer the yogurt cheese to a small bowl and stir in 1/4 teaspoon of pepper, the salt and 1 1/2 tablespoons of chives. Mound the cheese on a platter and, using a metal spatula, shape it into a disk about 5 inches across. Sprinkle the cheese with the remaining chives and pepper. Serve the yogurt cheese with the crackers.

Makes 4 servings

Note: The cheese can be covered with plastic wrap and refrigerated for up to 4 days, but the chive flavor will become more pronounced with time.

Yogurt Cheese with Pepper and Herbs, Buckwheat Crackers

BUCKWHEAT CRACKERS

Whole grains, green leafy vegetables, legumes and yeast are the major nonmeat sources of dietary molybdenum.

CALORIES per cracker	13
64% Carbohydrate	2 g
9% Protein	.3 g
27% Fat	.4 g
CALCIUM	3 mg
IRON	.04 mg
SODIUM	13 mg

1 cup buckwheat flour, approximately
1 cup unbleached all-purpose flour
1 tablespoon sugar
1/4 teaspoon baking soda
1/4 teaspoon salt
3 tablespoons margarine
2/3 cup plain lowfat yogurt

Preheat the oven to 325° F. Combine 1 cup of buckwheat flour, the all-purpose flour, sugar, baking soda and salt in a food processor. Add the margarine while pulsing the machine on and off for 15 seconds, or until the mixture resembles cornmeal. Add the yogurt and process for another 5 to 10 seconds, or until the mixture begins to form a ball of dough. (To mix the dough by hand, combine the dry ingredients in a large bowl and cut in the margarine, using a pastry blender or 2 knives. Add the yogurt and stir with a wooden spoon until the dough forms a ball and leaves the sides of the bowl.)

Divide the dough into 2 equal pieces. Dust the work surface and a rolling pin with buckwheat flour and roll out 1 piece of dough to a 10 x 10-inch rectangle about 1/16 inch thick. Prick the dough all over with a fork. Using a ruler and a sharp knife, cut the dough into twenty-five 2-inch squares, then cut them diagonally into triangles. Or, use a small cookie cutter to cut 50 crackers. Transfer the crackers to a baking sheet and bake for 20 minutes, or until crisp and slightly browned. Transfer the crackers to racks to cool and repeat with the remaining dough.   Makes 100 crackers

CAROB CHIP COOKIES

Eggs are a good source of selenium, which interacts with vitamin E as an antioxidant, protecting the body's tissues from the damaging effects of the oxidation of fatty acids.

Vegetable cooking spray
2 eggs
1 cup brown sugar
1 1/3 cups unbleached all-purpose flour
1/4 teaspoon baking powder
Pinch of salt
1 teaspoon grated orange peel
1/2 teaspoon orange extract
3/4 cup unsweetened carob chips (4 ounces)

Preheat the oven to 375° F. Spray a baking sheet with cooking spray; set aside. In a medium-size bowl beat the eggs and sugar until well blended. In a small bowl stir together the flour, baking powder and salt. Add the flour mixture, orange peel and orange extract to the egg mixture, and stir until the dry ingredients are just moistened. Stir in the carob chips. Drop the batter by rounded teaspoonsful about 1 1/2 inches apart on the baking sheet. Bake for 7 minutes, or until the cookies just begin to brown around the edges. (For chewier cookies, bake them for only 5 to 6 minutes.) Immediately transfer the cookies to racks to cool, then repeat with the remaining batter, spraying the baking sheet with cooking spray after every second batch. Store the cookies in an airtight container.   Makes 72 cookies

CALORIES per cookie	30
76% Carbohydrate	6 g
7% Protein	.6 g
17% Fat	.6 g
CALCIUM	5 mg
IRON	.2 mg
SODIUM	6 mg

PROP CREDITS

Cover: tank top, shorts, leotard, tights–Athletic Style, New York City; page 6: tank top, shorts–Athletic Style, New York City, leotard, bicycle shorts–Marika, San Diego, Calif., shoes–Nautilus Athletic Footwear, Inc., Greenville, S.C.; page 26: leotard crop top, shorts–Athletic Style, New York City, towels–Martex, New York City; pages 30-51: leotard, tights–Dance France, LTD, Santa Monica, Calif., T-shirt–Athletic Style, New York City, shorts–Naturalife, New York City, towel–Martex, New York City; pages 52-77: leotard, tights–Dance France, LTD, Santa Monica, Calif., shorts–Russell Corp., Alexander City, Ala., towel–Martex, New York City; page 78: camisole, pajama top–L'Affaire Lingerie, New York City; pages 82-97: rug–Einstein Moomjy, New York City, kilim pillows–Bokara Rug Co., Inc., New York City, taffeta pillows–B. Altman and Co., New York City; pages 98-123: camisole–L'Affaire Lingerie, New York City, rug–Einstein Moomjy, New York City, futon stand, futon, futon covering, pillows–The Futon Shop, New York City, vase courtesy of Lindsay Dimeo; page 126: tile–Nemo Tile, New York City; page 128: linen–Ad Hoc Softwares, New York City, chopstick rests, mug–Five Eggs, New York City, chopsticks courtesy of Lindsay Dimeo, plates–Sasaki, New York City; page 134: linens, flatware–Ad Hoc Softwares, New York City; plates–Platypus, New York City, salt and pepper shakers–Giles and Lewis, New York City; page 137: linen, pie knife–Ad Hoc Softwares, New York City, canisters–Conran's, New York City.

ACKNOWLEDGMENTS

All cosmetics and grooming products supplied by Clinique Labs, Inc., New York City

Nutrition analysis provided by Hill Nutrition Associates, Fayetteville, N.Y.

Off-camera warm-up equipment: rowing machine supplied by Precor USA, Redmond, Wash.; Tunturi stationary bicycle supplied by Amerec Corp., Bellevue, Wash.

Washing machine and dryer supplied by White-Westinghouse, Columbus, Ohio

Index prepared by Ian Tucker

Production by Giga Communications

PHOTOGRAPHY CREDITS

Exercise photographs by Andrew Eccles; food photographs by Steven Mays, Rebus, Inc.

ILLUSTRATION CREDITS

Pages 8, 11, charts, illustrations: Brian Sisco, Tammi Colichio; page 12, illustration: David Flaherty, chart: Brian Sisco; page 16, chart, illustration: Brian Sisco, Tammi Colichio; pages 20-21, 22: charts: Brian Sisco; pages 25, chart, illustration: Brian Sisco and Tammi Colichio.

Index